I) Every speech has a story

→ Purley's telling is one of
rhetorical context → time/Kairos is
the "So what?" → the Key

II) Chapter Break Down

4 & 5 are where it's @
close/textual analysis
→ what he does similar / what's unique

[Does not
waiver from
stance as a
rhetorical
critic]

III) This speech Keps adding
to its story, the legacy goes on

Abe:
→ Kennedy '63
→ Obama '08

→ The Narrative of this
speech continues to be telling,
as analysis of the 2008 election
comes in the VRA of '65
seems compelling

Library of Presidential Rhetoric

Martin J. Medhurst, General Editor

LBJ's American Promise

The 1965 Voting Rights Address

GARTH E. PAULEY

Texas A&M University Press : College Station

The paper used in this book meets the minimum requirements
of the American National Standard for Permanence
of Paper for Printed Library Materials, z39.48-1984.
Binding materials have been chosen for durability.

Frontispiece: Lyndon B. Johnson addresses
the U.S. Congress on March 15, 1965.
Courtesy Lyndon Baines Johnson Presidential Library.

Library of Congress Cataloging-in-Publication Data

Pauley, Garth E., 1971–
LBJ's American promise : the 1965 voting rights address /
Garth E. Pauley.—1st ed.
p. cm.—(Library of presidential rhetoric)
Includes bibliographical references and index.
ISBN-13: 978-1-58544-574-5 (cloth : alk. paper)
ISBN-10: 1-58544-574-6 (cloth : alk. paper)
ISBN-13: 978-1-58544-581-3 (pbk. : alk. paper)
ISBN-10: 1-58544-581-9 (alk. paper)
1. African Americans—Suffrage.   2. Voter registration—
United States.   3. Johnson, Lyndon B. (Lyndon Baines),
1908–1973—Oratory.
I. Title.   II. Title: Lyndon B. Johnson's American promise.
JK1924.O38   2007
324.6'208996073—dc22
2006021634

Contents

Acknowledgments

Although I cannot possibly thank everyone who helped me with this book, a number of people deserve special mention. First, I thank those colleagues who listened to or read earlier versions of this manuscript, especially Davis Houck, Moya Ball, Vanessa Beasley, and Steve Goldzwig. Second, I also thank the archivists and organizations that help preserve the nation's presidential history, especially archivist extraordinaire Allen Fisher and the LBJ Foundation, from which I received a generous grant in support of my research at the Lyndon B. Johnson Library. Third, I would like to express my gratitude to the trustees and supporters of Calvin College, which also provided generous support. Finally, I thank my wife, Kathi Groenendyk, and our two sons, Sean and Liam, for their patience, encouragement, and love during the research and writing of this book.

——————◆-•◆•-◆——————

Lyndon B. Johnson's
Special Message to the Congress

The American Promise

MARCH 15, 1965

Mr. Speaker, Mr. President, Members of the Congress:

I speak tonight for the dignity of man and the destiny of democracy.

I urge every member of both parties, Americans of all religions and of all colors, from every section of this country, to join me in that cause.

At times history and fate meet at a single time in a single place to shape a turning point in man's unending search for freedom. So it was at Lexington and Concord. So it was a century ago at Appomattox. So it was last week in Selma, Alabama.

There, long-suffering men and women peacefully protested the denial of their rights as Americans. Many were brutally assaulted. One *Rev R.* good man, a man of God, was killed.

There is no cause for pride in what has happened in Selma. There is no cause for self-satisfaction in the long denial of equal rights of millions of Americans. But there is cause for hope and for faith in our democracy in what is happening here tonight.

For the cries of pain and the hymns and protests of oppressed people have summoned into convocation all the majesty of this great government—this government of the greatest nation on earth.

Our mission is at once the oldest and the most basic of this country: to right wrong, to do justice, to serve man.

In our time we have come to live with moments of great crisis. Our lives have been marked with debate about great issues: issues of war and peace, issues of prosperity and depression. But rarely in any time does an issue lay bare the secret heart of America itself. Rarely are we met with a challenge not to our growth or abundance, our welfare, or our security, but rather to the values and the purposes and the meaning of our beloved nation.

The issue of equal rights for American Negroes is such an issue. And should we defeat every enemy, should we double our wealth and conquer the stars and still be unequal to this issue, then we will have failed as a people and as a nation.

For with a country as with a person, "What is a man profited, if he shall gain the whole world and lose his own soul?"

There is no Negro problem. There is no Southern problem. There is no Northern problem. There is only an American problem. And we are met here tonight as Americans—not as Democrats or Republicans—we are met here as Americans to solve that problem.

This was the first nation in the history of the world to be founded with a purpose. The great phrases of that purpose still sound in every American heart, North and South. "All men are created equal." "Government by consent of the governed." "Give me liberty or give me death." Well, those are not just clever words, or those are not just empty theories. In their name Americans have fought and died for two centuries, and tonight around the world they stand there as guardians of our liberty, risking their lives.

Those words are a promise to every citizen that he shall share in the dignity of man. This dignity cannot be found in a man's possessions; it cannot be found in his power or in his position. It really rests on his right to be treated as a man equal in opportunity to all others. It says that he shall share in freedom, he shall choose his leaders, educate his children, and provide for his family according to his ability and his merits as a human being.

To apply any other test—to deny a man his hopes because of his color or race, his religion or the place of his birth—is not only to do injustice, it is to deny America and to dishonor the dead who gave their lives for American freedom.

Our fathers believed that if this noble view of the rights of man was to flourish, it must be rooted in democracy. The most basic right of all was the right to choose your own leaders. The history of this country, in large measure, is the history of the expansion of that right to all of our people.

Many of the issues of civil rights are very complex and most difficult. But about this there can and should be no argument. Every American citizen must have an equal right to vote. There is no reason which can excuse the denial of that right. There is no duty which weighs more heavily on us than the duty we have to ensure that right.

Yet the harsh fact is that in many places in this country men and women are kept from voting simply because they are Negroes.

Every device of which human ingenuity is capable has been used to deny this right. The Negro citizen may go to register only to be told that the day is wrong or the hour is late or the official in charge is absent. And if he persists and if he manages to present himself to the registrar, he may be disqualified because he did not spell out his middle name or because he abbreviated a word on the application.

And if he manages to fill out an application he is given a test. The registrar is the sole judge of whether he passes this test. He may be asked to recite the entire Constitution or explain the most complex provisions of state law. And even a college degree cannot be used to prove that he can read and write.

For the fact is that the only way to pass these barriers is to show a white skin.

Experience has clearly shown that the existing process of law cannot overcome systematic and ingenious discrimination. No law that we now have on the books—and I have helped to put three of them there—can ensure the right to vote when local officials are determined to deny it.

In such a case our duty must be clear to all of us. The Constitution says that no person shall be kept from voting because of his race or his color. We have all sworn an oath before God to support and to defend that Constitution. We must now act in obedience to that oath.

Wednesday I will send to Congress a law designed to eliminate illegal barriers to the right to vote.

The broad principles of that bill will be in the hands of the Democratic and Republican leaders tomorrow. After they have reviewed it, it will come here formally as a bill. I am grateful for this opportunity to come here tonight at the invitation of the leadership to reason with my friends, to give them my views, and to visit with my former colleagues.

I have prepared a more comprehensive analysis of the legislation which I had intended to transmit to the clerk tomorrow but which I will submit to the clerks tonight. But I want to really discuss with you now, briefly, the main proposals of this legislation.

This bill will strike down restrictions to voting in all elections—federal, state, and local—which have been used to deny Negroes the right to vote.

This bill will establish a simple, uniform standard which cannot be used, however ingenious the effort, to flout our Constitution.

It will provide for citizens to be registered by officials of the United States government if the state officials refuse to register them.

It will eliminate tedious, unnecessary lawsuits which delay the right to vote.

Finally, this legislation will ensure that properly registered individuals are not prohibited from voting.

I will welcome the suggestions from all of the members of Congress—I have no doubt that I will get some—on ways and means to strengthen this law and to make it effective. But experience has plainly shown that this is the only path to carry out the command of the Constitution.

To those who seek to avoid action by their national government in their own communities, who want to and who seek to maintain purely local control over elections, the answer is simple.

Open your polling places to all your people.

Allow men and women to register and vote whatever the color of their skin.

Extend the rights of citizenship to every citizen of this land.

There is no constitutional issue here. The command of the Constitution is plain.

There is no moral issue. It is wrong—deadly wrong—to deny any of your fellow Americans the right to vote in this country.

There is no issue of states rights or national rights. There is only the struggle for human rights.

I have not the slightest doubt what will be your answer.

The last time a president sent a civil rights bill to the Congress it contained a provision to protect voting rights in federal elections. That civil rights bill was passed after eight long months of debate. And when that bill came to my desk from the Congress for my signature, the heart of the voting provision had been eliminated.

This time, on this issue, there must be no delay, or no hesitation, or no compromise with our purpose.

We cannot, we must not refuse to protect the right of every American to vote in every election that he may desire to participate in. And we ought not and we cannot and we must not wait another eight months before we get a bill. We have already waited a hundred years and more, and the time for waiting is gone.

So I ask you to join me in working long hours—nights and weekends, if necessary—to pass this bill. And I don't make that request lightly. For from the window where I sit with the problems of our country I recognize that from outside this chamber is the outraged conscience of a nation, the grave concern of many nations, and the harsh judgment of history on our acts.

But even if we pass this bill, the battle will not be over. What happened in Selma is part of a far larger movement which reaches into every section and state of America. It is the effort of American Negroes to secure for themselves the full blessings of American life.

[5]

Their cause must be our cause, too. Because it is not just Negroes, but really it's all of us who must overcome the crippling legacy of bigotry and injustice.

And we shall overcome.

As a man whose roots go deeply into Southern soil I know how agonizing racial feelings are. I know how difficult it is to reshape the attitudes and the structure of our society.

But a century has passed, more than a hundred years, since the Negro was freed. And he is not fully free tonight.

It was more than a hundred years ago that Abraham Lincoln, a great president of another party, signed the Emancipation Proclamation, but emancipation is a proclamation and not a fact.

A century has passed, more than a hundred years, since equality was promised. And yet the Negro is not equal.

A century has passed since the day of promise. And the promise is unkept.

The time of justice has now come. I tell you that I believe sincerely that no force can hold it back. It is right in the eyes of man and God that it should come. And when it does, I think that day will brighten the lives of every American.

For Negroes are not the only victims. How many white children have gone uneducated, how many white families have lived in stark poverty, how many white lives have been scarred by fear because we have wasted our energy and our substance to maintain the barriers of hatred and terror?

So I say to all of you here and to all in the nation tonight that those who appeal to you to hold on to the past do so at the cost of denying you your future.

This great, rich, restless country can offer opportunity and education and hope to all—black and white, North and South, sharecropper and city dweller. These are the enemies: poverty, ignorance, disease. They are the enemies and not our fellow man, not our neighbor. And these enemies too—poverty, disease, and ignorance—we shall overcome.

Now let none of us in any sections look with prideful righteousness on the troubles in another section or the problems of our neighbors.

There is really no part of America where the promise of equality has been fully kept. In Buffalo as well as in Birmingham, in Philadelphia as well as Selma, Americans are struggling for the fruits of freedom.

This is one nation. What happens in Selma or Cincinnati is a matter of legitimate concern to every American. But let each of us look within our own hearts and our own communities, and let each of us put our shoulder to the wheel to root out injustice wherever it exists.

As we meet here in this peaceful, historic chamber tonight, men from the South, some of whom were at Iwo Jima, men from the North who have carried Old Glory to far corners of the world and brought it back without a stain on it, men from the East and from the West are all fighting together without regard to religion, or color, or region in Vietnam. Men from every region fought for us across the world twenty years ago.

And now in these common dangers and these common sacrifices the South made its contribution of honor and gallantry no less than any other region of the great republic—and in some instances, a great many of them, more.

And I have not the slightest doubt that good men from everywhere in this country—from the Great Lakes to the Gulf of Mexico, from the Golden Gate to the harbors along the Atlantic—will rally now together in this cause to vindicate the freedom of all Americans. For all of us owe this duty and I believe that all of us will respond to it.

Your president makes that request of every American.

The real hero of this struggle is the American Negro. His actions and protests, his courage to risk safety and even to risk his life have awakened the conscience of this nation. His demonstrations have been designed to call attention to injustice, designed to provoke change, designed to stir reform.

He has called upon us to make good the promise of America. And who among us can say that we would have made the same progress were it not for his persistent bravery and his faith in American democracy?

For at the real heart of battle for equality is a deep-seated belief in the democratic process. Equality depends not on the force of arms or tear gas but depends upon the force of moral right, not on recourse to violence but on respect for law and order.

There have been many pressures upon your president, and there will be others as the days come and go. But I pledge you tonight that we intend to fight this battle where it should be fought: in the courts, and in the Congress, and in the hearts of men.

We must preserve the right of free speech and the right of free assembly. But the right of free speech does not carry with it, as has been said, the right to holler "fire" in a crowded theater. We must preserve the right to free assembly, but free assembly does not carry with it the right to block public thoroughfares to traffic.

We do have a right to protest and a right to march under conditions that do not infringe the constitutional rights of our neighbors. And I intend to protect all those rights as long as I am permitted to serve in this office.

We will guard against violence, knowing it strikes from our hands the very weapons which we seek—progress, obedience to law, and belief in American values.

In Selma as elsewhere we seek and pray for peace. We seek order. We seek unity. But we will not accept the peace of stifled rights, or the order imposed by fear, or the unity that stifles protest. For peace cannot be purchased at the cost of liberty.

In Selma tonight, as in every—and we had a good day there—as in every city, we are working for just and peaceful settlement. We must all remember that after this speech I am making tonight, after the police and the FBI and the marshals have all gone, and after you have promptly passed this bill, the people of Selma and the other cities of the nation must still live and work together. And when the attention of the nation has gone elsewhere, they must try to heal the wounds and to build a new community.

This cannot be easily done on a battleground of violence, as the history of the South itself shows. It is in recognition of this that men of both races have shown such an outstandingly impressive responsibility in recent days—last Tuesday, again today.

The bill that I am presenting to you will be known as a civil rights bill. But, in a larger sense, most of the program I am recommending is a civil rights program. Its object is to open the city of hope to all people of all races.

Because all Americans just must have the right to vote. And we are going to give them that right.

All Americans must have the privileges of citizenship regardless of race. And they are going to have those privileges of citizenship regardless of race.

But I would like to caution you and remind you that to exercise these privileges takes much more than just legal right. It requires a trained mind and a healthy body. It requires a decent home, and the chance to find a job, and the opportunity to escape from the clutches of poverty.

Of course, people cannot contribute to the nation if they are never taught to read or write, if their bodies are stunted from hunger, if their sickness goes untended, if their life is spent in hopeless poverty just drawing a welfare check.

So we want to open the gates to opportunity. But we are also going to give all our people, black and white, the help that they need to walk through those gates.

My first job after college was as a teacher in Cotulla, Texas, in a small Mexican American school. Few of them could speak English, and I couldn't speak much Spanish. My students were poor, and they often came to class without breakfast, hungry. They knew even in their youth the pain of prejudice. They never seemed to know why people disliked them. But they knew it was so, because I saw it in their eyes. I often walked home late in the afternoon, after the classes were finished, wishing there was more that I could do. But all I knew was to teach them the little that I knew, hoping that it might help them against the hardships that lay ahead.

Somehow you never forget what poverty and hatred can do when you see its scars on the hopeful face of a young child.

I never thought then, in 1928, that I would be standing here in 1965. It never even occurred to me in my fondest dreams that I might have the chance to help the sons and daughters of those students and to help people like them all over this country.

But now I do have that chance. And I'll let you in on a secret: I mean to use it. And I hope that you will use it with me.

This is the richest and most powerful country which ever occupied this globe. The might of past empires is little compared to ours. But I do not want to be the president who built empires or sought grandeur or extended dominion.

I want to be the president who educated young children to the wonders of their world. I want to be the president who helped to feed the hungry and to prepare them to be taxpayers instead of taxeaters.

I want to be the president who helped the poor to find their own way and who protected the right of every citizen to vote in every election.

I want to be the president who helped to end hatred among his fellow men and who promoted love among the people of all races and all regions and all parties.

I want to be the president who helped to end war among the brothers of this earth.

And so at the request of your beloved Speaker and the senator from Montana; the majority leader, the senator from Illinois; the minority leader, Mr. McCulloch; and other members of both parties, I came here tonight—not as President Roosevelt came down one time in person to veto a bonus bill, not as President Truman came down one time to urge the passage of a railroad bill—but I came down here to ask you to share this task with me and to share it with the people that we both work for. I want this to be the Congress, Republicans and Democrats alike, which did all these things for all these people.

Beyond this great chamber, out yonder in fifty states, are the people that we serve. Who can tell what deep and unspoken hopes are in their hearts tonight as they sit there and listen. We all can guess, from our own lives, how difficult they often find their own pursuit of happiness, how many problems each little family has. They look most of all to themselves for their futures. But I think that they also look to each of us.

Above the pyramid on the great seal of the United States it says—in Latin—"God has favored our undertaking."

God will not favor everything that we do. It is rather our duty to divine His will. But I cannot help believing that He truly understands and that He really favors the undertaking that we begin here tonight.

Transcribed from an audio recording of the speech held in the archives of the Lyndon B. Johnson Library. President Johnson's Voting Rights Address, March 15, 1965, WHCA 269/70, Audio Collection, Lyndon B. Johnson Library.

Introduction

Experts in history, politics, and law often argue about how to rank Lyndon B. Johnson's presidency, offering different summary judgments of his peculiar combination of skills and deficiencies in the areas of congressional leadership, foreign policy management, political vision, domestic governance, and administrative ability. But few, if any, would argue that Lyndon Baines Johnson—LBJ—was one of the United States' better presidential orators. As a speaker, Johnson often appeared affected and ill at ease: His pacing was clumsy, his voice monotonous, his physical expression awkward, and his articulation poor. Although his mother taught elocution lessons and he himself had taught public speaking in Cotulla and Houston, Texas, LBJ seemed in practice ignorant to most of the basic principles of effective oratory. His shortcomings as a presidential orator stemmed from his failure to study and practice the techniques of successful speakers, his discomfort with the electronic media, and his preference for private rather than public persuasion. In many of his speeches, LBJ seemed fixed behind the podium and stuck to his speaking script, detached from his immediate and televised audiences, and unable to transfer his considerable interpersonal communication skills to the public forum.

Yet President Johnson was capable of oratorical success. In his televised address soon after the assassination of John F. Kennedy, LBJ effectively eulogized his predecessor and demonstrated continuity in the federal government. And when addressing the issue of racial justice, Johnson sometimes exhibited genuine eloquence. During a 1964 campaign speech in New Orleans, he extemporized the civil rights section of his address, presenting an anecdote to emphasize that Southerners should not allow race baiters to obscure their interests or divide them from the Democratic Party: He narrated the story of an aging Southern senator who told Congressman Sam Rayburn (D-Texas) that the citizens of Louisiana needed to hear a genuine Democratic speech because "All they ever hear at election time is nigra, nigra, nigra." The tale represented Johnson's persuasion at its best—frank, heartfelt, and a little earthy. These features, combined with his personal identification with the South throughout the message, brought about an animated ovation after the initial shock caused by the president's language subsided. These compelling and uniquely Johnsonian rhetorical qualities also distinguish another of LBJ's eloquent messages on civil rights, a speech that stands as his greatest oratorical triumph—his voting rights address of March 15, 1965.

Johnson delivered this civil rights message in response to two exigencies: first, the public outcry against the intensive demonstrations in Selma, Alabama, and second, his own desire to sign a strong voting rights measure into the books of law. The voting rights protests in Selma, stepped up by Martin Luther King Jr. on January 2, 1965, had succeeded in exposing to Americans some of the worst instances of voter disfranchisement and intimidation in the nation. In addition, the violence committed by Alabama law enforcement officials and local citizens in order to maintain white rule—especially the extreme violence perpetrated against demonstrators on Sunday, March 7—led many Americans to call for immediate federal intervention and executive action. During several press conferences, LBJ and his aides had spoken publicly about the protests in Selma, but the president's March 15 speech was his first sustained response to the crisis and his first statement that satisfied many citizens' desire for a tough, explicit

public message. The speech also expressed his commitment to ensuring
that Congress enacted a meaningful voting rights statute, a commitment that some had previously questioned, though Johnson had been
working behind closed doors since the summer of 1964 to develop a
legislative solution to the problem of voter discrimination against
African Americans.

Johnson's speech was historic and emphasized the historical urgency
and gravity of the civil rights crisis then facing the nation. LBJ was
the first president since Harry Truman to deliver in person a special
message to Congress on a piece of domestic legislation. Beginning at
9:02 P.M., he spoke to the congressmen and senators assembled in the
House chamber of the capitol and to a televised audience of about seventy million Americans. His primary goals were to formally announce
his intention to seek a legislative solution to the problem of African
American voter disfranchisement, to demonstrate the need for such a
solution, to outline the features of the administration's voting rights
bill, and to urge the Congress to pass that measure quickly. However,
Johnson's speech did more—much more. LBJ claimed that the present civil rights crisis represented a critical trial of national character,
testing whether "the American promise" would be extended to all of its
citizens. He lauded civil rights protestors for helping the nation make
progress toward fulfilling that promise, and he voiced his own strong
commitment to racial progress by declaring in the speech's surprising
climax the anthem of the civil rights movement, "We shall overcome."
Finally, he connected the issue of racial progress to an expansive vision of an educated, healthy, economically secure, independent, and
compassionate American citizenry.

President Johnson's "We Shall Overcome" speech was well received
in its own time and remains highly regarded. The day after he delivered his message, Martin Luther King Jr. called it "the most moving,
eloquent, unequivocal, and passionate plea for human rights ever made
by a president of this nation." Moreover, nearly thirty-five years later,
a survey of leading public address scholars ranked LBJ's speech as one
of the top ten American speeches of the twentieth century.[1] Johnson's
speech is remarkable because it is demanding; because it is personal,

both in his identification with the South and with the oppressed; because it expresses lofty national ideals in ordinary language; because it acknowledges the failures of the past and present yet remains hopeful about the future; because it represents thoughtful engagement with the issue of civil rights for African Americans; and above all because it symbolically leverages a temporary moment of public acuity to the problem of voting rights to achieve an important, long-lasting public good. In addition, the president's serious, firm delivery communicated his resolve and determination. The speech has its flaws, to be sure: LBJ spoke too slowly, expressed grandiose ideas at times, and became rather self-absorbed near his conclusion. Nonetheless, this address stands as his finest and as one of the most significant episodes in twentieth-century political rhetoric in the United States. The speech expresses the maturation of his thinking on the issue of racial justice and superbly frames the issue of voting rights—perhaps the primary civil right in a democratic society—in order to enable reflective political deliberation and decision making mindful of the urgency of the moment. The text is remarkable for its clarity, its conviction, its compassion, and its compelling claims—in short, because it possesses the qualities of the best political oratory.

My purpose in this book is to provide a full account of Johnson's "We Shall Overcome" speech, accounting for the president's decision to speak; the preparation and revision of the address; the speech's responsiveness to historical events and its effort to symbolically frame its historical contexts; the speech's argument, structure, language, style, and values; the persona LBJ assumed in delivering his message; the audiences to whom the address is directed and those to whom it does not speak; and its effects and impact. Significant attention has already been granted to Johnson's speech: It is included or excerpted in scores of published anthologies that chronicle the "great moments" or "great issues" of U.S. history, and nearly every biography of Lyndon Johnson and almost every history of the civil rights struggle discusses this speech.

Nevertheless, most of the attention thus far given to the speech has provided little more than a static, documentary context for understanding it. As such, President Johnson's address has been reduced to an index of public opinion at that time about voting rights, or to an expression of the nation's long-standing commitment to expand the right to vote, or to a marker of the U.S. presidency's expanding commitment to racial justice. In addition, commentaries on Johnson's speech that proclaim its greatness offer little more than the synoptic content analysis or simple interpretations of its rhetorical force: For instance, biographer Robert Dallek suggests that LBJ's address is "one of the most moving and memorable presidential addresses in history" because of its drama and idealism, and biographer Robert Caro suggests that the speech is powerful and a "high-water mark of the tides of social justice" because it contains ringing language, expresses the president's determination, and took the case of civil rights further than it had ever gone before.[2]

The judgments of both historians are right, as far as they go. President Johnson's message is eloquent in part because it possesses the qualities that each author identifies; later in this book I flesh out their judgments but essentially agree with their basic conclusions. At the same time, many speeches possess these qualities yet are not deemed landmarks of American oratory. To justify proclaiming this particular address to be a milestone, there must be parity between interpretation and an overall judgment of rhetorical significance. To capture the greatness of Johnson's "We Shall Overcome" speech more fully, we must evaluate it on grounds appropriate for judging the use of the spoken word to assign meaning and to persuade others to share that meaning. As a document, Johnson's message is significant because it was spoken by a significant historical figure at a significant historical moment about a significant historical problem. However, as a speech, it is striking because of LBJ's (and his speechwriters') capacity to find persuasive appeals appropriate to the issue, the moment, and the audience and to deploy them effectively. To judge this or any speech—*as a speech*—to be great, one must carefully analyze the dynamic symbolic interaction between speaker, subject, context, and listener. The central aim of this book is to do just that.

While studying the rhetorical appeal of Johnson's voting rights address, we must also view it through the lens of politics. President

Johnson was an excessively political man, and his speech to Congress and the nation was an instance of calculated political action: It was part of a comprehensive campaign to pass voting rights legislation that included public pressure and behind-the-scenes maneuvering, negotiating, and brokering for power. My account of LBJ's speech examines the politics of voting rights while focusing on how this political issue was made salient, meaningful, and in a sense real through persuasive communication.

Because this book has political rhetoric as its subject, it is a book about politics in action—that is, politics created in the public space between speaker, subject, context, and listener. The ideas LBJ expressed on March 15 were shaped, driven, and warranted by the demands of political action. Johnson's speech provided affirmation, challenge, vision, and hope, and the chapters to come examine the ways in which the president's address affected his relationship with civil rights activists and shaped public perceptions of the possibilities of government-led social change. Chiefly this book investigates the way in which Lyndon Johnson made the principle of equal voting rights meaningful and compelling through a public vocabulary of shared interests, motives, and aspirations in order to secure passage of the United States' most important civil rights law.

The following chapters pursue different threads that aid our understanding of Johnson's speech but weave them into a cohesive account. The complex configuration of events, ideas, and people to which LBJ's speech belongs is made up of interrelated parts that must be examined separately to perceive them clearly and also in relation to the whole to see them completely.

A helpful point of entry into this configuration is the history of voting rights in the United States. Rather than aiming for completeness, chapter one focuses on the constitutional, legal, and political wrangling related to voting by racial minorities, primarily African Americans. Constitutional amendments, court rulings, state constitutions, and voting registrar practices form an important context for understanding President's Johnson's March 15 address. His speech locates voting rights in an expansive, as well as an immediate, historical context: He deplores both the failure to guarantee blacks access to the ballot box and the historical and contemporary practices used by state and local officials to keep African Americans from voting. He points out the failure of previous laws to secure the right to vote, and he suggests that the trajectory of U.S. history has generally been aimed at extending the right to vote to all people. LBJ's speech is marked by a sense of history, one that must be understood to develop an informed interpretation of his message.

The historical wrangling over voting by African Americans intensified in 1965, when leaders of the civil rights movement decided to make securing the franchise through federal legislation their chief goal. Chapter two chronicles the 1965 voting rights campaign, with brief reference to earlier movements. The demonstrations in Selma, Alabama, were the most significant development in this drive, and thus I focus on the events there, but other efforts by civil rights activists at that time to secure political power also deserve attention. The dynamic context comprised of voting rights protests, voter registration practices, violence, public opinion, and court rulings was the central influence on Johnson's decision to address the nation and on the purpose, language, tone, and argument of the speech itself. In addition, the text of the address suggests a particular way of understanding the demonstrations, which makes examining them from a historical perspective vital to interpreting President Johnson's message. Moreover, since LBJ had in January of 1965 encouraged civil rights leaders to undertake a campaign of exposing the worst instances of voter discrimination, examining the demonstrations in Selma will provide a helpful perspective for interpreting the president's response to such a campaign once activists actually enacted it in the unpredictable, ominous political milieu in Selma.

Though the Selma demonstrations were the critical element of the political process that brought about the enactment of a new voting rights statute, the U.S. Justice Department—at Johnson's request—had begun preparing legislation prior to the protests there. Chapter three provides a short administrative history of the White House's voting rights bill, beginning with the germination of the measure in 1964 and ending with its formal proposal by the president in March of 1965. The drafting of the legislation was weighted by concerns related to necessity, feasibility, efficacy, constitutionality, and expedience. The legislative suggestions made by civil rights leaders and the dynamics of public opinion triggered by their protests shaped the drafting process: The administration struggled to meet the leaders' demands, to finalize its bill quickly, and to avoid appearing forced into action. At the same time, however, the White House also wanted to draft the measure carefully to ensure that it would pass, work, and be upheld by the courts. LBJ's March 15 speech justifies the need for voting rights legislation, justifies the administration's particular approach to solving the problem of black disfranchisement, and explains the provisions of the nearly completed bill. An understanding of the proposed law's administrative history and features, then, is necessary to interpret Johnson's justifications and explanations. We must also examine the timing of the proposal's drafting, as it influenced the timing of the president's speech.

Johnson waited until the bill was finished (except for a few final adjustments) to address the joint session of Congress and the nation. Chapter four investigates his decision to speak publicly on the evening of March 15, his discussions with his staff and members of Congress about the speech's timing and content, the drafting of the message by speechwriters, and Johnson's revision of the address. We will see that LBJ was sensitive to the rhetorical situation surrounding the civil rights crisis and attempted to formulate discursive responses that he perceived to be prudent, fitting, and timely.

Johnson's rhetorical attentiveness is evident in his "We Shall Overcome" speech. Intimating that the need for voting rights legislation is as self-evident as the right it seeks to secure, he urges his listeners to show their good judgment by supporting the measure. The historical and contemporary warrants he constructs bolster his argument for equal access to the ballot box. In justifying immediate action, he suggests that the present does not represent a moment of frenzy but rather a moment of historical gravity in which the United States must demonstrate its character. He implies that what will emerge from this moment is not merely a resolution to the conflict of voices and political interests but also justice. His discussion of the provisions of the bill is not so detailed that it might drain power from the potent symbol of "voting rights." While doing all of this, he speaks to the diverse listeners who compose the audience. Chapter five undertakes a close analysis of Johnson's speech, including the way in which he used the available means of persuasion to influence his audience and thus historical events. We examine how and how well LBJ used the tools of rhetoric—language, organization, narrative, explication, definition, interpretation, and argument—in the constraining circumstances in which he spoke. The significance and meaning of the address is to be found in his words, ideas, and their presentation, as well as in how those features interact with the dynamic of events, people, and issues of which his speech was a part.

As one of his most significant public messages, President Johnson's voting rights address received tremendous public attention. Most listeners praised the speech, and civil rights activists, politicians, and historians later judged it to be a major influence on the quick passage of voting rights legislation. Chapter six considers the commentaries, reactions, and political outcomes that LBJ's message provoked. I am interested in the straightforward opinions and valuations his audience offered—which can reveal important attitudes—but am more concerned with what the responses reveal about the persuasiveness and impact of his claims. For example, repetition of Johnson's language, application of his definitions, and deployment of his narrative as a frame for judgment in the reactions to the speech and subsequent public messages on voting rights would stand as evidence of its influence. In short, I examine the way in which the comments on Johnson's speech reveal the president's ability to reconfigure the moment of national preoccupation with African American disfranchisement and how that reconfiguration impacted the political process.

After analyzing (with some measure of independence) the elements of the historical configuration to which LBJ's speech belongs, I conclude the book with a perspective on the whole, discussing the relationships not fully explicated through an examination of the parts in their chronological order. In an important sense, the reality of communication exists in the flow of changing circumstances of which the communication is a part.[3] Examining the whole of the rhetorical context and its dynamics is thus important for making sense of the individual speech act—in this case, Lyndon Johnson's voting rights address. In closing, I also reconsider the significance of his speech today for those interested in the rhetoric, history, and politics of the United States.

CHAPTER ONE

America's Voting Rights Problem

Nearly eight minutes into the delivery of his "We Shall Overcome" speech, Lyndon Johnson claimed that the history of the United States is by and large the history of the expansion of the right to vote "to all of our people." LBJ's idealistic statement suggested that the current of history was on his side, but it also simplified the contested history of suffrage in the United States. Johnson's sense of history is a common one inasmuch as many Americans (and foreigners) infer that the trajectory of voting rights in the United States has been straight, steady, and always aimed at universal suffrage since the Revolution. Actual progress toward expanding the franchise, however, has come in fits and starts, and episodes that restricted the privilege are as common as those that extended it. By exploring this winding path of voting rights history, we can better understand and evaluate Johnson's construction of a historical argument for the Voting Rights Act of 1965. This exploration passes through five historical periods, beginning with the nation's founding and ending with the civil rights revolution of the 1960s. My aim throughout is to reveal the broader context that occasioned and shaped President Johnson's speech and to provide the basis for determining whether his depiction of the past is accurate, full, and completely persuasive.

Founding

During the House Judiciary Committee hearings on Watergate in 1974, Barbara Jordan (D-Texas), who was black, reflected on her commitment to the Constitution: "But when that document was completed, on the seventeenth of September in 1787, I was not included in that *We the people*. . . . But through the process of amendment, interpretation, and court decision I have finally been included in *We the people*." Jordan's reflection on her exclusion from what James Madison called "the great body of the people of the United States" is accurate if for no other reason than that the Constitution viewed most blacks, who were slaves, "in the mixed character of persons and property."[1] However, the Constitution did not fully bar African Americans from political participation as part of "We the people" since it did not prohibit them from voting: The Constitution left voting requirements to the individual states, and, in the eighteenth century, blacks who met property qualifications in the Northern states voted alongside whites. Even though it took the Voting Rights Act of 1965 to make possible Barbara Jordan's election, the Constitution did not proscribe such an electoral outcome prior to its amendment and interpretation.

It is a peculiarity of history that the United States, which, in declaring its independence, claimed that the government derives its "just powers from the consent of the governed," did not originate an electorate in its constitution. Article I of the Constitution grants Congress the power to regulate the times, places, and manner of federal elections but not the authority to determine voter qualifications. Under the Constitution of 1787, the states, rather than the federal government, created the voter, although this creation was wholly authorized by and subject to the national constitution. Historian Alexander Keyssar notes that the Constitution "left the federal government without any clear power or mechanism, other than through constitutional amendment, to institute a national conception of voting rights, to express a national vision of democracy."[2] The Revolutionary rhetoric of natural rights and representative government that echoed in LBJ's voting rights speech (and most African American protest rhetoric) did not make its way into the Constitution's clauses on voting. Although the Constitution did not contain the universal manhood suffrage clause advocated by a few of the Revolutionaries, it did not prohibit blacks (or others whose fitness for voting was deemed questionable at that time) from voting in principle, but it did exclude most blacks from voting in effect, given the voter qualification laws in place in most states. Well into the twentieth century, the relegation of suffrage qualifications to the states remained a source of frustration to African Americans who demanded equal access to the ballot box: In addition to battling over the civil rights issue, advocates had to demonstrate that solutions to the problem of disfranchisement would not upset the federal-state relationship suggested by the Constitution.

However, had the framers included a uniform suffrage clause in the Constitution, they might have created a smaller electorate than that authorized by state suffrage laws. Several important members of the Constitutional Convention, including John Dickinson of Delaware and Robert Morris of Pennsylvania, supported restricting the franchise to "freeholders," citizens who owned property. Believing only land ownership to be constitutive of a vested interest in the community, advocates of restricted suffrage believed freeholders were the best "guardians of liberty." Other supporters of the freehold restriction noted that the common people had not voted wisely during the postwar period and had revealed their nasty distemper during Shays's Rebellion.[3]

Opponents of the freehold qualification argued that the common people deserved to exercise the rights and privileges of citizenship: During the Constitutional Convention, Virginian George Mason claimed that common folk were equally worthy of "being trusted with the common rights of their fellow Citizens"; Nathaniel Gorham of Massachusetts argued that electoral outcomes in Boston, New York, and Philadelphia, in which merchants and mechanics voted, were "at least as good as those made by freeholders only"; and Pennsylvanian Benjamin Franklin argued that the Revolutionary War had revealed "the virtue and public spirit of our common people" and thus their fitness for voting. Nevertheless, practical arguments (rather than those raised by Mason, Gorham, and Franklin) seem to have headed off moves to restrict the franchise. Most members of the convention seemed persuaded by a type of argument advanced by several representatives but stated most clearly by Connecticut delegate Oliver Elsworth, who claimed that "the people will not readily subscribe to the National Constitution" should it disfranchise them through suffrage laws more restrictive than those of their own state. As an apparent compromise to ensure ratification, the authors of the Constitution avoided writing a uniform suffrage clause.[4]

Anyone who seeks to analyze constitutional arguments on voting rights must understand that the framers of the Constitution did not resolve the issues of fitness for voting, voting rights, and the authority of the federal government to establish voter qualifications. The members of the Constitutional Convention did not view every person as fit for voting; only a small number believed voting was a natural right rather than a privilege conferred by the state, and few argued that a federal government did not have the power to establish a universal suffrage clause. Furthermore, although a committee of detail brokered a compromise on franchise qualifications to avoid angering citizens in states with few restrictions on the ballot (which would threaten ratification), the framers did not consider another alternative—designing a franchise clause more generous than that of any of the states. The Constitution's failure to state in positive terms who constituted the electorate was made worse by its failure to define who constituted the citizenry. The Founding Fathers implicitly excluded the progenitors of Barbara Jordan from membership in "We the People," but the Constitution of 1787 guaranteed no one membership in that group. Federal law did not define citizenship until the passage of the Civil Rights Act of 1866 and the ratification of the Fourteenth Amendment.[5]

Reconstruction

The Civil Rights Act of 1866, enacted by Congress in April (over President Andrew Johnson's veto), was the first statutory definition of the rights of U.S. citizenship. The act established that "all persons born in the United States and not subject to any foreign power, excluding

Indians not taxed, are declared to be citizens" and that no state law or custom could deprive U.S. citizens of their fundamental rights as free men, rights possessed regardless of race. The act was significant because it created a national conception of citizenship and gave meaning to the Thirteenth Amendment, defining in legislative terms the essence of freedom. Still, the statute had a significant shortcoming with regard to voting: Inasmuch as the act was mute about the specific political rights of African Americans, it remained true to the tradition that voting was a privilege rather an essential attribute of citizenship.[6]

Passed by Congress in June 1866 and ratified in July 1868, the Fourteenth Amendment to the Constitution eliminated doubt as to the constitutionality of the Civil Rights Act: In declaring that all natural-born or naturalized persons "are citizens of the United States and the State wherein they reside," it confirmed both the primacy of national citizenship and that African Americans were citizens. The amendment also prohibited states from enacting or enforcing laws that "abridge the privileges or immunities of citizens of the United States" and from denying to any person "the equal protection of the laws." These provisions had significant implications for voting, as citizenship was a necessary prerequisite for exercising the franchise. Moreover, the stipulations intimated that denial of the franchise on the basis of race might constitute denial of equal protection. The amendment also addressed the issue of voting more specifically in providing for a reduction in a state's congressional representation in proportion to the number of male citizens to whom the suffrage "is denied . . . or in any way abridged." Congressional advocates of the amendment hoped it would grant the franchise to African Americans in the South, but they pursued a peculiar path to confer access to the ballot box. By trying to pressure the Southern states into letting African Americans vote rather than guaranteeing blacks the franchise, the amendment implicitly acknowledged the right of states to limit voting because of race. In short, the amendment was, in the words of legal scholar Richard Claude, "a clumsy substitute for an outright grant of Negro suffrage."[7] For African Americans who wanted to vote, the shortcomings of the Fourteenth Amendment were that it did not firmly establish that the right to vote is a privilege necessarily accompanying citizenship, that it did not guarantee the right of suffrage, and that it relied on the federal judicial process for enforcement.

Beginning in March of 1867, after the passage of the Fourteenth Amendment but prior to its ratification, Congress took a more direct approach to enfranchising African Americans in the states of the former Confederacy. The Reconstruction Acts of 1867 declared that in order to free themselves from military rule and be fully readmitted to the Union, the Southern states had to approve by manhood suffrage constitutions that allowed blacks to vote on equal terms with whites and ratify the Fourteenth Amendment. These measures enfranchised nearly one million African Americans in the South, many of whom demonstrated their enthusiasm for political participation at the soon-convened state conventions and elections and in new political organizations.[8]

Though the Reconstruction Acts were crucial to the political consciousness and the mobilization of African Americans, they too had significant limitations. Perhaps most importantly, the commitment to black suffrage contained in the measures applied only to the South. In addition, although not a problem of the language of the laws themselves, the dominant Republican ideology that led to their passage held that, once accorded equal rights, blacks would, in the words of historian Eric Foner, "find their social level and assume responsibility for their own fate."[9] As such, many congressional lawmakers had unrealistic expectations of the Reconstruction Acts, believing that guaranteeing African Americans the franchise alone would settle the "Negro question" and the problem of federal intervention in the South since blacks would soon gain sufficient political power by exercising this new right. These utopian expectations about the power of the right to vote to guarantee to African Americans full political self-determination persisted long after the Reconstruction era and were expressed by many twentieth-century civil rights activists and President Lyndon Johnson.

The Fifteenth Amendment to the Constitution went further than its immediate predecessor toward guaranteeing African Americans access to the ballot box. Even though the amendment became the constitutional focus of most subsequent voting rights advocacy and legislation, including the Voting Rights Act of 1965, it did not actively confer the right to vote. Rather, the amendment prohibited the federal and state governments from depriving any citizen of the franchise "on account of race, color, or previous condition of servitude." Although it constitutionally altered the implicit suggestion of the Fourteenth Amendment that the states could limit voting because of race, it still suggested that voting was a privilege that states could regulate in other ways. Demonstrating keen foresight, some congressional advocates of black suffrage decried the Fifteenth Amendment as inadequate; they believed that Southern states would establish voter qualifications that were not racially discriminatory prima facie but were nonetheless designed to exclude African Americans from voting. However, two key concerns prevented the adoption of a broader amendment that would have prevented such exclusions and expanded the definition of citizenship for all Americans. The first was a belief among lawmakers that a broad voting amendment would undermine the autonomy and authority of the states by giving the federal government the power to create the voter. The second was the desire of many Northern lawmakers and their constituents to allow for nonracial voter discrimination against some whites on the basis of age, residence, education, ethnicity, property, and religion. These two concerns—and a peculiar political process that culminated in a surprising legislative compromise by a conference committee—helped produce a Fifteenth Amendment that opened the door to literacy tests, poll taxes, and property qualifications in the South that were intended to disfranchise blacks.[10] The narrow amendment passed by Congress in February 1869 and ratified in March 1870 did not meet many congressional Republicans' expectations for expanding the franchise, for guaranteeing the right of African Americans to hold office, or for establishing uniform voting requirements across the nation.[11]

Congress could not rest after passing the Fourteenth and Fifteenth Amendments, however, because the Ku Klux Klan and similar groups initiated a campaign of terror in the South designed to prevent blacks from exercising their new political rights. Congress responded by enacting the Enforcement Acts of 1870–71. These laws forbade state election officials from discriminating against voters on the basis of race, authorized the president to appoint election supervisors who had the power to bring cases of voter discrimination to federal court, and designated certain civil rights crimes—namely, conspiracies to deprive citizens of the right to vote, hold office, serve on juries, and enjoy equal protection of the law—as offenses punishable under federal law. With the passage of the Enforcement Acts, the major burden of suppressing racial violence fell to the federal government. And the government did take action to produce a dramatic decline of violence in the South by 1872, which enabled hundreds of thousands of African Americans to vote and elect black candidates to local, state, and federal offices.

The Supreme Court soon issued rulings that weakened the Enforcement Acts, however, and helped establish a voting climate in the South marked by violence, intimidation, obstruction, and fraud. In 1875 the high court declared in *Minor v. Happersett* that "the Constitution of the United States does not confer the right of suffrage upon any one" and that "the privilege of voting is derived not from the United States but is conferred by the state."[12] This ruling suggested that states might confer or deny the right to vote at will, except as limited by the Fifteenth Amendment's ban on racial discrimination; it ushered in an era of Southern-state voting laws that did not discriminate by race prima facie but were designed to keep African Americans from voting, as forecast by proponents of a broader Fifteenth Amendment.

In 1876 Supreme Court rulings in *United States v. Cruikshank* and *United States v. Reese* suggested that, in order to secure convictions in voter discrimination or intimidation cases, federal attorneys must prove that the offenders both operated as agents of the state and intended to discriminate for reasons of race. In their insistence upon proving intentionality and in guaranteeing state jurisdiction for private citizens accused of voter discrimination, these two rulings made the successful prosecution of electoral fraud virtually impossible. Southern legislatures moved to exclude black voting by enacting statues that did not, in their actual wording, reveal their racially discriminatory intent. Collectively, the Supreme Court's decisions made it difficult to control the racial violence, intimidation, poll taxes, and other less visible means used by Southern whites to "redeem" their political power.[13] Moreover, the court decisions, as well as the withdrawal of federal troops from the South in 1878, helped create an environment in which Southerners used discriminatory qualifications to prevent African Americans from registering, turned to violence and intimidation to depress black voter turnout, and used fraud to undo the effect of votes still cast.

Redemption

Despite the thoroughly discriminatory voting climate in the South during the post-Reconstruction era, some African Americans still managed to vote and participate in electoral politics during the 1870s and 1880s. However, Southern whites plotted to shrink the black electorate through gerrymandering, discriminatory registration systems, complicated ballot configurations, secret ballots, and fraudulent vote counts; when these failed, racist whites often turned to intimidation and violence. The end of this period of black voter participation coexisting with efforts at exclusion began in 1890.

A central event that signaled the end of black electoral participation was Congress's failure to pass the Federal Elections Bill, referred to by its opponents as the Lodge Force Bill. The legislation sought to expand and strengthen the Enforcement Acts of the 1870s: It authorized federal circuit courts—on petition from a small number of citizens from any district—to appoint federal supervisors of congressional elections and permitted federal officials and the courts to overturn election results that state officials had declared and certified. In January 1891 the measure's defeat in the Senate brought congressional efforts to enforce the Fifteenth Amendment to a halt and signaled to the South that the federal government was not prepared to act energetically to guarantee blacks' voting rights. Congress did not consider federal intervention into Southern politics to realize the Fifteenth Amendment until it debated the Johnson administration's voting rights bill in 1965.[14]

In this new voting rights climate, Southern legislatures passed new election laws in the 1890s that were not discriminatory at face value, with Mississippi leading the way. New tools to keep blacks from casting their ballots in the Magnolia State included residence requirements, literacy and understanding tests, and poll taxes. Other states soon followed suit, adopting similar measures and new ones, including the disqualification of voters who did not have vouchers of "good character" and who had committed crimes of "moral turpitude." Southern states also moved to exclude African American voters through the adoption of grandfather clauses, which exempted male citizens from voter qualification requirements if they or their ancestors had been able to vote prior to the ratification of the Fifteen Amendment, and white primaries, which sought to evade the Constitution by limiting voting in primary elections to members of state political parties (asserted to be private organizations that thus could conduct elections and establish qualifications for their members as they saw fit). The net effect of these efforts was the disfranchisement of nearly all black citizens in the South by 1910; moreover, by that year the Southern states had expelled nearly all African American legislators from office. During this time, the Supreme Court upheld the legality of all of the major techniques of disfranchisement, most notably in *Williams v. Mississippi*, in which the high court declared that the state's constitution and voter qualification laws did not "on their face discriminate between the races."[15]

Scheming

From the 1910s to the 1940s, the Supreme Court issued rulings that undermined some of the discriminatory voting laws and constitutional provisions, and some Southern states abolished the poll tax on their own initiative. However, just as racist whites did not intend the end of the poll tax to enfranchise African Americans (indeed they did not abolish it for this purpose), they did not plan to let court rulings on techniques of disfranchisement put ballots back in the hands of black citizens. Instead, white supremacists developed new voter discrimination measures to get around the high court's decrees immediately following unfavorable rulings. This series of blocks and end runs around the law slowed the progress of voter equality and took a toll, timewise and financially, on African Americans who wanted to vote.

The political contest related to the grandfather clause clearly illustrates the scheming in regard to voter qualification laws that marked
this era. In 1915 the Supreme Court suggested that grandfather clauses
violated the Fifteenth Amendment. In *Guinn v. United States,* the high
court ruled that such a clause in Oklahoma had been adopted to give
whites who might otherwise have been disfranchised by the state's
literacy test a way of qualifying to vote unavailable to blacks and thus
represented unconstitutional voter discrimination on the basis of race.
It declared that, although "it contains no express words of an exclusion
from the standard which it establishes of any person on account of
race, color, or previous condition of servitude, prohibited by the 15th
Amendment," the grandfather clause "inherently brings that result
into existence since it is based purely upon a period of time before the
enactment of the 15th Amendment."[16]

In response, the Oklahoma legislature drafted a new grandfather
clause that exempted citizens who voted in 1914—before the *Guinn*
ruling—from the state's literacy test. This tactic was invalidated by
the Supreme Court but not until 1939, in its ruling in *Lane v. Wilson.*
The majority opinion in this case sent a strong message to states who
sought to avoid the requirements of the Fifteenth Amendment by developing cleverly worded voting laws that were not—in the estimate
of those states—racially discriminatory at face value. Justice Felix
Frankfurter declared, "The Amendment nullifies sophisticated as well
as simple-minded modes of discrimination. It hits onerous procedural
requirements which effectively handicap exercise of the franchise by
the colored race although the abstract right to vote may remain unre-
stricted as to race."[17]

The history of the white primary also illustrates the scheming
undertaken by Southern states to maintain white supremacy in
electoral politics. The creation of the white primary itself was a
machination devised to circumvent the Fifteenth Amendment by
shifting racial discrimination from general to primary elections,
which, given the dominance of the Democratic Party in the South,
was the election of consequence. The Supreme Court initially upheld
this system, declaring in the 1921 case *Newberry v. United States* that

the party primary was separate from the election process and was thus not protected by the Constitution. Six years later in *Nixon v. Herndon,* the high court declared that a Texas statute that prohibited blacks from voting in the Democratic primary violated the Fourteenth Amendment since the state acted in a manner to deprive African Americans of equal protection by controlling the primary election. The Texas legislature attempted to maintain its white primary, however, by decreeing that every political party could prescribe the voter qualifications of its own members, thus shifting the act of racial discrimination to the Texas Democratic Party. The party's executive committee quickly declared that only whites could vote in its elections.

In 1932 the Supreme Court voided this arrangement, too, decreeing in *Nixon v. Condon* that the new white primary was unconstitutional since it was still an integral, state-authorized part of the electoral system. However, Justice Benjamin Cardozo suggested a way to undermine the effect of the court's ruling: In his majority opinion, he stated that political parties could legally bar blacks if the discrimination were enacted by state conventions rather than executive committees. Within two weeks, the Texas Democratic Party followed Cardozo's implicit suggestion; the party convention declared that all white citizens were eligible for membership and thus refused to distribute ballots to African Americans.

Nonetheless, the white primary began to unravel following the Supreme Court's ruling in *United States v. Classic.* Although this 1941 case did not address racial discrimination, it did call into question whether primary elections were subject to federal control. Reversing its decision in *Newberry,* the court decreed that the right to vote in primary elections was protected by the Constitution "where the state law has made the primary an integral part of the procedure of choice, or where in fact the primary effectively controls the choice" of the federal election.[18] This ruling also dealt a blow to the "state derivation" doctrine of voting expressed in *Minor v. Happersett,* as it declared that the right to vote—not just the right to be free from voter discrimination—is protected by the Constitution. In the 1944 case *Smith v. Allwright,* the

Supreme Court applied the reasoning of the *Classic* case to the racial discrimination in party primaries and declared that electoral choice "is not to be nullified by a State through casting its electoral process in a form which permits a private organization to practice racial discrimination in the election. Constitutional rights would be of little value if they could thus indirectly be denied."[19] The court thus concluded that the white primary violated the Fifteenth Amendment. Not all Southern segregationists immediately gave up on the white primary, however: After the *Smith v. Allwright* ruling, a few Southern states cleared their books of any reference to party primaries, hoping to remove primary elections from state control in the eyes of the law. Nonetheless, in 1947 the Fourth Circuit Court of Appeals declared this arrangement unconstitutional and thus finally put an end to the white primary.

The progress toward equal voting made in the early twentieth century, however, was limited. The end of the grandfather clause had little impact on African American voting, as other measures still kept blacks from casting their ballots. The end of the white primary did lead to a surge in their electoral participation after 1947, but they still faced significant obstacles. White supremacists responded to their losses in the Supreme Court by focusing on other means of voter discrimination: gerrymandering, the unfair application of literacy and understanding tests, slow processing of blacks' voter registration forms, relocation of polling places without prior notification to African Americans, voucher systems, delay tactics to make appeals impossible, registration of a few blacks on occasion to keep out of federal court, purgation of African American voters from the rolls, and intimidation of would-be black voters. In a column for the *Pittsburgh Courier*, African American journalist J. A. Rogers effectively summed up the situation during this era: "Each time the United States Supreme Court outlaws one of these 'Negro stoppers,' a new one is invented."[20] As a consequence of this cycle, many voting rights advocates began to believe that action by the other two branches of the federal government was necessary to enforce the rights guaranteed by the Fourteenth and Fifteenth Amendments.[21]

Uprising

From the late 1940s to the mid-1960s, voting rights advocates received some measure of support from the White House and the federal legislature. Each president during this era urged an end to voter discrimination, and, with presidential support, Congress passed three civil rights laws before 1965 that contained voting rights provisions. But not each president applied the full weight of his office to finally secure equal access to the ballot box, and the laws Congress produced during this era still forced African Americans to seek remedy for voter discrimination in the courts.

In his public and private messages, Harry Truman voiced his support for ending voter discrimination against African Americans. Claiming that every American should have "the right to an equal share in making the public decisions through the ballot," he called for strong, "effective Federal action" to "protect the civil rights of its citizens," especially the right to vote, as recommended in 1948 by the President's Committee on Civil Rights.[22] Moreover, strong federal support was needed during Truman's presidency. The Supreme Court's decision in *Smith v. Allwright* both brought an end to the white primary and heightened fury at Southern resistance to African American voting. White supremacists applied literacy and understanding tests with new zeal; local law enforcement officials were more antagonistic; and election officials used their power more arbitrarily to exclude blacks. Whites threatened blacks on the eve of elections and sometimes murdered those, including Georgia war veteran Isaac Nixon in 1948, who voted anyway. However, although President Truman was a solid advocate of racial justice and believed that the federal government could take expansive action to ensure equal rights, he did not provide strong leadership on the problem of voter discrimination. In his February 1948 special message on civil rights, he urged Congress to enact legislation "to give qualified citizens Federal protection of their right to vote" but did not invest much political capital in the fight for legislation.[23] As a consequence of this failure and the inability to overcome obstructionist tactics by Southern legislators, Congress did not pass voting rights legislation during the Truman years.

During the presidency of Dwight Eisenhower, another Supreme Court decision increased Southern whites' resistance to African American voting. The court's 1954 ruling in *Brown v. Board of Education* was a powerful blow to Jim Crow in that it helped dismantle segregated schooling in the South by declaring that "in the field of public education the doctrine of 'separate but equal' has no place."[24] The decision also triggered a backlash that led many Southern white supremacists to see any political action by African Americans as a significant threat to their way of life. In 1954 White Citizens' Councils organized to thwart desegregation and included voter discrimination as part of their campaign to ensure white supremacy. In addition to the usual methods of voter discrimination, the councils urged more comprehensive action: They arranged for employers to threaten to fire black employees who planned to register to vote and for banks to foreclose on the mortgages of black voters. As a consequence of these efforts, black voter registration declined in the South, and many African Americans lost the will to vote. Voter registration efforts by civil rights organizations stalled, and it became clear to many voting rights advocates that federal legislation was necessary to tear down the wall of Southern resistance to African American voting.

Although Eisenhower had expressed some support for the principle of equal voting rights during the 1952 campaign, his administration demonstrated no interest in pursuing a legislative agenda to secure those rights until 1955. In the fall of that year—prompted by increased racial violence, the spread of White Citizens' Councils, and pressure from legislators and civil rights groups—the Justice Department began to reevaluate its legislative stance on civil rights problems. After reviewing the department's investigative reports, Attorney General Herbert Brownell directed its Civil Rights Section to prepare new legislative recommendations, which upon completion included provisions to abate the problem of voter discrimination in the South. The bill prepared by the Justice Department contained a variety of civil rights provisions, but Brownell emphasized the one advocated most strongly by the president, referring to it as "a voting rights bill." Protecting the right to vote fit the administration's desire to avoid direct federal intervention in civil rights disputes: Expressing a logic similar to that of supporters of the Reconstruction Acts, Eisenhower claimed that the vote would provide the black citizen with "the means of taking care of himself and his group."[25] Many civil rights activists, including Martin Luther King Jr., expressed similar sentiments during the campaign for voting rights legislation. At the May 17, 1957, Prayer Pilgrimage for Freedom, King made an appeal: "Give us the ballot, and we will no longer have to worry the federal government about our basic rights."[26]

The legislation that ultimately became the Civil Rights Act of 1957 was weakened by a series of legislative compromises brokered by Lyndon Johnson, then serving as Senate majority leader. Even though Johnson, too, believed the vote would allow African Americans to secure other civil rights for themselves, his political ambitions and desire to pass the first civil rights act since Reconstruction led him to render the bill's voting rights provisions ineffective. Title IV of the bill aimed to significantly strengthen the federal government's ability to prosecute election officials and citizens who stood between blacks and the polls by authorizing the attorney general to seek injunctions and file suits in cases of voter discrimination. However, in order to avoid a Southern filibuster, Johnson maneuvered to add a jury-trial amendment to the bill, which guaranteed that the accused who violated a federal injunction and were cited for criminal contempt would be tried by a jury of local citizens. The amendment made the legislation's voting rights provision nearly meaningless, as most Southern juries were unlikely to convict defendants engaged in the campaign against black voting. President Eisenhower spoke out clearly against this compromise: He stated that jury trial "should not be interposed" between a court order and its enforcement and claimed that passing such an amendment would be tantamount to "welcoming anarchy."[27]

Nonetheless, the watered-down bill passed Congress, and the president signed it into law on September 9, 1957. The Civil Rights Act of 1957 was a weak measure because of the jury-trial amendment, which emboldened election officials in the South to continue discriminating against African Americans, and because it placed the burden of enforcement on a Justice Department that lacked the will and the full capability to enforce it.[28] But the law did contain two significant provisions that ultimately helped secure the right to vote. Title II made the Civil Rights Section of the Justice Department a full-fledged division, and Title I created the United States Commission on Civil Rights (USCCR).

Soon after its creation, the USCCR pursued voting rights complaints, held hearings on voter discrimination, and conducted field investigations in states where black voter registration and participation were suspiciously low. In 1959 the commission published a report that showed the persistence of thorough voter discrimination against African Americans in the South. It reveals as mistaken those who suggest that Southern legislators let a voting rights bill pass in 1957 because they and their constituents felt some measure of constitutional guilt about denying blacks the right to vote. Putting the problem of voter discrimination into historical perspective, the 1959 report observed, "The history of voting in the United States shows, and the experience of this Commission has confirmed, that where there is will and opportunity to discriminate against certain potential voters, ways to discriminate will be found." The commission noted that Southern segregationists denied blacks the franchise "through the creation of legal impediments, administrative obstacles, and positive discouragement engendered by fears of economic reprisal and physical harm." It claimed that the litigation required by existing civil rights laws was both slow and ineffective and that the existing laws did not address many of the voter discrimination schemes common in the South. The commission emphasized that "new legislation is needed." Its findings and recommendations echoed those of the Southern Regional Council, which in 1959 also urged federal legislation to end the purges, slowdowns, refusals, tests, and threats that still kept most African Americans in the South from voting.[29]

With support from President Eisenhower, the Justice Department began drafting new civil rights legislation in January 1960 to make further strides in securing African Americans' access to the ballot box. In his 1960 State of the Union address, the president urged the nation to protect "the right to vote . . . against all encroachment."[30] However, the administration's legislative proposal was grounded in the belief that the federal courts could expand the suffrage, a belief that by 1960 seemed dubious to most voting rights advocates. The Civil Rights Act of 1960, a slightly altered version of the White House bill, provided a few additional weapons for the court battles over voter discrimination. The measure permitted the attorney general to seek a federal district court ruling that a "pattern or practice" of voter disfranchisement existed in a particular locale. If the court issued such a ruling, the district court judge could then select voter referees to determine whether the African American plaintiffs qualified to voter under state law; if qualified, the plaintiffs would be issued a certificate to vote, and the appointed referees would oversee the polls to ensure compliance. The law also contained provisions to frustrate new delaying tactics used by Southern states and required states to retain their election records for twenty-two months and make them available to the attorney general for inspection.

Even though the 1960 act passed in part because of prodding from the U.S. Commission on Civil Rights, it did not institute the commission's recommendation to authorize federal registrars to administer elections in areas that, according to the district courts, discriminated by race in the exercise of the franchise. The act's provision for locally appointed referees rather than federally appointed registrars gave the Southern states a good deal of control over their discriminatory electoral systems. In addition, the act relied on Southern district court judges for fair enforcement overall. Moreover, since it was based on the legislation passed three years earlier, the Civil Rights Act of 1960 possessed the shortcoming of relying on the slow process of litigation to address the pervasive problem of voter discrimination against Southern African Americans.

During the first two years of his presidency, John Kennedy focused on executive action, negotiation, persuasion, and litigation as the means to solve civil rights problems rather than pursuing legislative solutions. Although he voiced his opposition to the "denial of constitutional rights to some of our fellow Americans on account of race—at the ballot box and elsewhere,"[31] he did not propose measures to solve the shortcomings of the Civil Rights Acts of 1957 and 1960. Reflecting the White

House's preferences, Attorney General Robert Kennedy announced that his department would take a more activist stance combating voter discrimination than it had during the Eisenhower administration. The Justice Department secured victories in federal cases against many of the formal practices used to bar blacks from voting, including the rejection of registration forms because of minor errors and omissions, voucher systems, and laws that applied discriminatory rules to both races once most whites were registered. However, the Justice Department found it more difficult to secure convictions in cases of voter harassment and intimidation. And despite these legal victories, most African Americans in the South still could not vote: Litigation had limited success in the areas where the cases were won, did not induce other areas to comply voluntarily, and moved too slowly to secure widespread access to the ballot box. In 1961 the U.S. Commission on Civil Rights reported that a discriminatory electoral process and threats of violence and economic reprisal prevented most Southern blacks "from exercising their right to vote." The commission recommended that Congress enact legislation prohibiting all voter qualifications other than age, residence, confinement, and felony conviction.[32]

By 1962 the president's public messages suggested that he believed further legislation was necessary to address the problem of voter discrimination. For instance, in his 1962 State of the Union address, President Kennedy emphasized that the right to vote "should no longer be denied through such arbitrary devices . . . as literacy tests and poll taxes."[33] The White House soon proposed legislation to end the poll tax, which ultimately took the form of a constitutional amendment, and supported a measure to end the unfair application of literacy tests. The anti–poll tax measure succeeded and became the Twenty-fourth Amendment, but the literacy test bill died in Congress due in part to tepid backing from President Kennedy. In 1963 the attorney general persuaded his brother that the administration should pursue legislation to secure equal access to the ballot box for Southern blacks. In a January report to the president, Bobby Kennedy claimed that "Additional legislation is necessary to insure prompt relief . . . where the facts indicate that substantial numbers of Negroes are being deprived of the right to register and vote because of race." In a special message to Congress just a month after receiving this report, the president called for legislation to end the discriminatory "judicial delay" and "administrative abuse" that characterized the electoral process in most Southern states.[34]

The White House's proposed civil rights legislation contained modest voting rights provisions: It focused on expediting the judicial process, providing for voter registration while cases were being heard, and reforming the application of literacy tests. As a result of the nature of civil rights activism in 1963 (especially the protests in Birmingham, the desegregation of the University of Alabama, and the March on Washington), the public accommodations, employment, and education provisions of the proposal overshadowed those pertaining to voting rights. During the summer and fall of 1963, the Kennedy administration worked to secure passage for its civil rights bill, but the president died from an assassin's bullet before Congress voted on the measure.

Immediately after assuming the presidency on November 22, 1963, Lyndon Johnson developed a strategy to ensure the passage of President Kennedy's civil rights bill. Through a campaign that demonstrated a keen sensitivity to the national mood, legislative acumen, bargaining ability, and rhetorical skill, LBJ goaded Congress to enact a civil rights measure even stronger than that introduced by his predecessor. The Civil Rights Act of 1964, which became law on July 2, remained moderate in its voting rights provisions, however. The law barred election officials from applying different standards and procedures to blacks when determining voter qualifications, prevented the disqualification of registrants for errors or omissions immaterial to their substantive qualifications for voting, ordered literacy tests to be administered in writing and to be made available in advance, declared that a sixth-grade education must be accepted as evidence of literacy, aimed to reduce the time of litigation in suits filed by the attorney general, and provided for a special three-judge court to hear suffrage cases while court cases against election officials awaited resolution.

The 1964 act did not contain the tough remedies the USCCR claimed were necessary to end voter discrimination. In its 1963 report, the commission emphasized the shortcomings of the legal proceedings approach to ending voter discrimination: "The reasons for the low rate of increase in Negro registration appear to include the high cost of litigation, the slowness of the judicial process on both the trial and appellate level, [and] the inherent complexity of supervising the enforcement of decrees." The report also observed that discriminatory application of literacy tests, constitutional interpretation tests, requirements to prove good character, voucher systems, discrimination in providing assistance to voter applicants, failure to notify applicants of rejection, and intimidation and reprisal still barred most blacks in the South from voting. The USCCR claimed that "drastic change in the means used to secure suffrage" were necessary. The commission recommended legislation that allowed the president to appoint registrars to enroll qualified African Americans as voters in both federal and state elections and prohibited election officials from rejecting voter applications for any reason other than age, residency, or literacy (established by a nondiscriminatory standard). It also recommended that Congress invoke Section II of the Fourteenth Amendment to reduce the congressional representation of the states that persisted in discriminating against black citizens.[35]

Though the Civil Rights Act of 1964 was a significant legislative improvement over the 1957 and 1960 Civil Rights Acts—as it contained important measures to help end racial discrimination that had been excised from those previous acts—it did not fill in the gaps of those earlier acts with regard to voting. Indeed, in 1964 most civil rights advocates believed that Title I of the law was outmoded and would do little to improve the status of black voting in the South. The Johnson administration saw the 1964 law's limitations in regard to voting even before its passage: In June 1964 a White House task force stated that "the bill still leaves the States with considerable ability to evade the intent to provide for the registration of Negro voters" and that significant improvement in black electoral participation would require "direct federal intervention, either administratively or legislatively."[36]

By 1964, despite the enactment of federal legislation to enforce the Constitution's provisions on voting, pervasive racial discrimination continued to thwart the guarantees of the Fifteenth Amendment.[37]

Even though existing laws and the court decisions obtained under them theoretically made it more difficult for states to keep African Americans disfranchised, the slowness of litigation and the perpetual process of election officials switching to discriminatory devices not covered by law or decree rendered the law largely ineffective. Before the passage of the Voting Rights Act of 1965, only one-third of voting-age blacks in the states covered by the law were registered to vote, and Southern resistance to African American voting remained strong and effective.

Conclusion

Lyndon Johnson's simplification of the contested history of suffrage in his "We Shall Overcome" speech is understandable inasmuch as that history is long, winding, and complex. Though the Founding Fathers believed the franchise was the ultimate safeguard of liberty and the foundation of republican governance, they did not establish voter qualifications or an electorate in the Constitution. Congress attempted to clarify these questions of citizenship and the electorate during Reconstruction. Federal legislation and constitutional amendments aimed to include more African Americans as voters but did so only in the South, not by granting citizens equal rights and often in a clumsy manner. Indeed, during the period referred to as Redemption, white supremacists took advantage of the amendment's inadequacies. Although the era began with a legislative effort to expand and strengthen previous civil rights measures and enforce the Fifteenth Amendment, it was marked primarily by systematic efforts in the South to end African American electoral participation in a manner deemed constitutional. When the courts declared some of these discriminatory practices unconstitutional in the era I refer to as Scheming, Southern states switched (sometimes following hints from judges) to new practices not covered by the law.

In response to these problems, the executive and legislative branches took action to curb voter discrimination during the period I call Uprising. Nevertheless, these efforts had limited impact since, for success, they depended on the slow, often ineffective process of litigation. At the beginning of 1965 there existed in much of the South a fierce will to deny blacks the franchise and a strong, flexible system of fraud, intimidation, and reprisal. Each was supported by the long history of voter discrimination and the nation's inability to decisively secure equal access to the ballot box for African Americans.

Also at this time, civil rights organizations seemed more motivated than ever to win the struggle over the vote, which had always been at the heart of the movement; strong federal voting rights legislation seemed possible; the courts appeared supportive of federal efforts to end voter discrimination according to race; and the nation's president seemed determined to secure equal voting rights, a determination expressed most eloquently in LBJ's address to Congress and the nation on March 15.

President Johnson's "We Shall Overcome" speech is animated by its sense of U.S. history and the Constitution. He urges the nation to grant African Americans "the most basic right" valued by the Founding Fathers and to heed "the command of the Constitution." However, the Voting Rights Act was much more than a fulfillment of the political rights established by the Founders and codified in the Constitution. Many U.S. politicians and political thinkers of the 1780s did not possess a commitment to universal suffrage or believe that voting was a natural right. As a living document, the Constitution evolved in its conception of the right to vote (e.g., from a right derived from the states to one authorized by the Constitution) as a result of its amendment and interpretation. The commitment to equal voting contained in the Voting Rights Act did not just symbolize the fulfillment of the Fifteenth Amendment, which sought simply to free citizens from voting discrimination on explicitly racial grounds; rather, it was a commitment to expand the definition of citizenship to include African Americans and to deepen the meaning of the constitutional provisions on voting. Despite language that hides its rhetorical nature, LBJ's voting rights speech does not simply hold up the Constitution as a template and call for an end to all voting practices that are not visible within the cut pattern; moreover, it does not merely describe a map of the winding path of voting rights history and allow the audience to infer the next stop. Instead, the speech interprets the values of the Constitution and history, gives them new meaning, and adapts them to the sociopolitical context of 1965. Indeed, from this process Johnson's speech draws its rhetorical force.

Understanding the history of voting rights and voter discrimination in the United States provides us with a stable vantage point for surveying the contours of President Johnson's "We Shall Overcome" speech. The meaning of his address resides in large part in the history that occasioned it. For example, we can interpret his claim that the Founders' philosophy of voting rights constitutes an endorsement of his bill, his assertion that the mandate of the Constitution on the issue of voting is clear, his contention that previous laws failed to ensure the right to vote, and his depiction of the devices of voter discrimination only if we understand the speech's broader historical context. At the same time, we must also understand another, more immediate element of the historical context that occasioned and shaped the president's message—the 1965 voting rights campaign, especially the protests in Selma, Alabama.

CHAPTER TWO

Battling for the Ballot

Although Lyndon Johnson was proud of the Civil Rights Act of 1964, he recognized the law's limitations and believed that only a measure guaranteeing equal access to the ballot box would fully undermine the Southern structures of racial discrimination. Believing in the primacy of the right to vote, Johnson called it "the basic right without which all others are meaningless" and claimed that the ballot was "the most powerful instrument . . . for breaking down injustice."[1] As an enactment of these beliefs, the president encouraged civil rights advocates to focus the citizenry's attention on the problem of voter discrimination in the South, hoping that their efforts would function as a catalyst for the enactment of voting rights legislation. When demonstrations helped make the issue of electoral discrimination an urgent social problem in 1965, LBJ credited African Americans in his "We Shall Overcome" speech. He claimed that the protestors in Selma—not the president—had "summoned into convocation all the majesty of this great government" and lauded them for urging the nation to "make good the promise of America," the assurance of political freedom and equality before the law.

The demonstrations in Selma, Alabama, helped bring into being the United States' most significant voting rights law and shaped the timing, arguments, and language of President Johnson's March 15 address. As such, they form an important context for evaluating the text. For example, we must understand the events in Selma in historical terms in order to judge LBJ's interpretation of those events in his voting rights message. We must understand the public sentiments triggered by the Selma demonstrations to evaluate how the president appeals to those feelings. We must understand the system of voter discrimination in Selma—and how civil rights activists exposed that system to the public—to determine whether Johnson's discussion of voting rights legislation seemed appropriate to the circumstances. And we must understand the reasons the voting rights activism in Selma succeeded in eliciting a strong rhetorical response from the president, whereas previous campaigns had not transformed the issue of voter discrimination into a public and political crisis. In short, exploring the context of the voting rights movement will help us appreciate its dynamics, especially the way in which it interacts with political and rhetorical action, including Johnson's "We Shall Overcome" speech.

Prologue

President Johnson rightly praised civil rights demonstrators in his "We Shall Overcome" address for bringing the nation to a moment of historical reckoning, but his discourse omits any reference to voting rights activism before 1965. Though the Selma protests brought the issue of black voting rights to its apex, activism between the mid-1940s and early 1960s made the Selma campaign possible and demonstrated African Americans' patience, resolve, and courage in their efforts to secure the franchise.

The initial step in African Americans' mobilization with regard to the vote came in 1944, following the Supreme Court's decision in *Smith v. Allwright*. After the court effectively ended the white primary in its April ruling, African American voter registration burgeoned, spurred by organizations dedicated to increasing black electoral participation. For example, the National Progressive Voters League, the NAACP, and the Regional Council of Negro Leadership initiated suffrage drives to register African American citizens. The NAACP and the Highlander Folk School organized citizenship schools to educate Southern blacks about the electoral process. In addition, politically active blacks formed local voter leagues that educated the citizenry, organized registration campaigns, endorsed candidates, shaped voting blocs, and encouraged participation at the polls. The outcomes of these organized campaigns demonstrated that many African Americans were interested in voting, that they could mobilize for political participation, and that a combination of national and local organizations could effectively mobilize potential voters.

Although these campaigns significantly increased the number of blacks registered to vote, still less than twenty percent of qualified African Americans in the South were registered to vote by 1952.[2] Following initial efforts to mobilize, the white backlash still depressed African American electoral participation, as did a lack of time, money, knowledge, economic freedom, and interest among some blacks, which kept them from developing a strong desire to vote. Still, although the campaigns of this era did not produce a significant shift in political power in the South, they were an important step in priming African Americans for electoral participation.

Voter organizations persisted in the late-1950s, and civil rights organizations, led by the NAACP, also stepped up their efforts to battle voter discrimination by lobbying for federal civil rights legislation. Nevertheless, as chapter one points out, the legislation passed during this era—the Civil Rights Acts of 1957 and 1960—had little impact on the entrenched system of racial discrimination that characterized the Southern states' electoral systems. As a result of their disappointment with the watered-down provisions enacted through the NAACP's lobbying efforts, some blacks began to question the association's legislative tactics, which emphasized behind-the-scenes negotiation rather than mobilization of the black masses into provocative action.[3]

Nonetheless, one part of the lobbying effort supported by the NAACP included mass protests and presaged the tactics used by civil rights activists in the 1960s: the Prayer Pilgrimage for Freedom. On March 17, 1957, nearly twenty-seven thousand demonstrators converged on the Lincoln Memorial in Washington, D.C., to demand among other things the passage of strong voting rights provisions as part of the Civil Rights Act of 1957. The moderate tone of the event and the relatively calm political climate in which it was undertaken kept the pilgrimage from capturing the attention of Congress or eliciting a rhetorical response from President Eisenhower, another of the organizers' goals. The rally did demonstrate, however, that civil rights groups could organize a large-scale demonstration, and it primed some African Americans for direct nonviolent action.

Though the civil rights laws that were passed during the Eisenhower administration disappointed voting rights advocates, their desire to register black citizens and provoke change remained strong: Indeed, many activists' interpretation of the Civil Rights Acts of 1957 and 1960 as a "half loaf" and "first step" raised their expectations and spurred them on. Eager to channel this energy into moderate activities that did not produce political crises—as had direct protest in the areas of public accommodations and interstate transportation, such as the Freedom Rides—the Kennedy administration steered some civil rights activism toward enfranchisement activities by helping to provide for massive voter registration drives. White House officials persuaded philanthropic organizations to underwrite an organized effort to register African Americans and research the causes of black voter disfranchisement. The Voter Education Project (VEP) began in 1962, with civil rights workers traveling to communities across the South to stimulate black electoral participation. Their persistence and dedication yielded increases in the number of African Americans registered to vote: Nearly seven hundred thousand blacks—almost all of whom lived in counties that the VEP canvassed—qualified to vote for the first time. The project also connected local blacks with national organizations, helped establish and energize local voter groups, and produced voting statistics that the federal government later used in its efforts to fight voter discrimination. Yet the VEP offensive did not burst or even seriously crack the dam of discrimination that stopped the stream of black voters in the South. The project's gains in voter registration came mostly in cities and states in which African Americans could already vote without too much obstruction or fear of retaliation; it had little effect in areas of hard-core resistance, such as Alabama and Mississippi. Violence against civil rights workers, retaliation against local blacks, and new tools of voter discrimination prevented the VEP from producing a larger increase in black voting. Despite the limited nature of the gains they produced, voting rights activists persisted in their commitment to expanding the black electorate through education and registration campaigns.

In 1963, black Mississippians working together under the Council of Federated Organizations (COFO) developed a unique, intensive voting movement aimed at demonstrating that African Americans would vote if given the chance, educating black citizens, establishing local political organizations, and mocking the legitimacy of the regular state election. The Freedom Vote campaign held its own statewide political convention, nominated and rallied support for its own candidates for Mississippi governor and lieutenant governor, and staffed polling places where blacks could vote in this mock election. Voting rights workers overcame intimidation, harassment, and other efforts to disrupt the vote: More than 83,000 African Americans participated, but that number fell far short of the COFO planners' goal of securing 200,000 black ballots. In addition, the operation did not receive significant attention from the national news media. In addition, more than two-thirds of the ballots cast in the Freedom Vote came from just eight counties in the state. As a result of these failures, civil rights organizers in Mississippi began to plan for a larger voter education and registration project, one that would reach into additional communities, focus more on statewide (rather than grassroots) organizing, and generate national publicity.[4]

Strongly committed to developing black electoral participation in the Magnolia State, the coordinators organized a voting drive for the summer of 1964 that revealed the strengths and weaknesses of education and registration campaigns. During Freedom Summer, volunteers moved into nearly every African American community in Mississippi to educate local citizens, register them to vote, organize them into a political party, and marshal support for the party's candidates. Significant numbers of white volunteers participated in Freedom Summer, but some black activists, especially more militant members of the Student Nonviolent Coordinating Committee (SNCC), were antipathetic or opposed to white involvement. Mississippians committed to white political supremacy, however, did not make racial distinctions and threatened both white and black voting rights workers with violence: Indeed, one of the first acts of violence against Freedom Summer volunteers was the murder of James Chaney, who was black, and Michael Schwerner and Andy Goodman, who were white. Throughout the summer, activists and local residents endured arrests, shootings, bombings, and beatings. Despite this context of strong opposition and confrontation, Freedom Summer succeeded in educating many local blacks about the political process, instilling in them a new resolve to assert their right to the ballot, and organizing them into the Mississippi Freedom Democratic Party (MFDP). The movement also gave civil rights workers important community organizing experience and left behind new or strengthened local voter groups in many communities. However, the summer campaign failed to destabilize the structures of white supremacy that sustained Mississippi politics—an outcome that dispirited many activists. Still, the drive increased in small measure national awareness of the pervasive discrimination that existed in the South. But because the violence during Freedom Summer was often less conspicuous and spectacular than that provoked by nonviolent direct action and not immediately connected to the act of voting itself, it did not transform the issue of voter discrimination into a national political crisis.

The initial political mobilization of African Americans following *Smith v. Allwright*, the lobbying effort for federal legislation, the Voter Education Project, the Freedom Vote, and Freedom Summer was a necessary antecedent to the voting rights campaign of 1965. This movement developed the local groups, the connections with national organizations, the level of political education, the desire, the boldness, the reluctant and often calculated cooperation with whites, and the experience necessary to make possible a voting rights campaign that would transform politics in the South.

Selma: Foundation

The voting rights activism in Selma that reached its apex in March 1965 had its roots in a campaign initiated by SNCC more than two years earlier. At the end of 1962, Bernard Lafayette, a veteran of the Nashville student movement and the Freedom Rides, toured Selma to consider the city for inclusion in SNCC's voter registration project in the deep South. He found a long-standing but weak voter organization—the Dallas County Voters League (DCVL)—and resistance to the idea of registering by many local blacks, but Lafayette still settled on Selma as the site for his voting rights assignment, seeing the project as a personal challenge. In February 1963 he returned to Selma and initiated his campaign to promote voter registration. He and other SNCC workers, including his wife, Colia, canvassed black neighborhoods and rural areas to discuss voting rights and emphasize the importance of the franchise. They also helped the DCVL set up citizenship classes, protest marches, and mass meetings. Moving quickly to try to end this "outside agitation" in the county seat, Dallas County sheriff Jim Clark lashed out physically against marchers, arrested activists, and often stationed himself and his lawmen inside the places where local blacks met. Local whites joined the effort to crush the budding voting rights movement: They threatened the workers, assaulted them, and fired African American teachers who participated in the campaign. Retaliation weakened the efforts in Selma, but a core group of blacks from the community, especially Amelia Boynton, Marie Foster, Frederick Reese, and James Gildersleeve, remained committed to the cause. Though Lafayette left Selma in September to resume his studies at Fisk University and to await the birth of his first child, SNCC workers continued to canvass the African American community, arrange mass meetings, and coordinate voter registration efforts.[5]

A turning point in the drive to increase black voter registration in Selma came on "Freedom Day"—October 7, 1963. Three hundred fifty African Americans lined up outside the Dallas County courthouse to register to vote, even though the local election board had never registered more than thirty or forty applicants per day. Hoping to register, the citizens had begun assembling around 9 A.M. but were soon surrounded by a law enforcement contingent, which then grew in number throughout the day. Sheriff Clark and his deputies used nightsticks to keep SNCC workers moving; they arrested three blacks who raised protest signs on the steps of the federal building across from the courthouse; they kept prospective registrants from leaving the line to use the bathroom and prevented voting rights workers from bringing them food or drink. The situation was tense: Those standing in line were steadfast yet anxious; those patrolling them were angry and on edge. Violence soon erupted. At about 2 P.M. Clark and his men attacked two SNCC field secretaries—Chico Neblett and Avery Williams—as they tried to bring food and drink to those standing in line: The officers knocked the two men to the ground, beat them, seared them with cattle prods, and then arrested them. Law enforcement officials assaulted the men in plain view of the journalists and celebrities (including writer James Baldwin and entertainer Dick Gregory) invited by SNCC to witness the strong resistance to black voting in Alabama—and in front of four FBI agents and two Justice Department attorneys. Local black citizens continued to wait outside the courthouse until 4:30 P.M., when the election board closed its doors, having processed fewer than ten percent of the applicants waiting in line. Despite their frustrations, the activists expressed feelings of triumph at a mass meeting that night: That so many African Americans had attempted to register and not faltered in the face of violence was deemed a major accomplishment. In his speech that evening, SNCC executive secretary James Forman told the activists they had achieved "something great" by standing up to Jim Clark. Freedom Day emboldened the black community in Selma.[6]

This achievement, however, was inadequate to the task of routing white hegemony in local elections or focusing national politics on the issue of disfranchisement. The burgeoning movement showed white Selma its determination and secured some attention from the press but did not generate an urgent public, congressional, or presidential demand for a strong remedy to the problem of African American disfranchisement.

Local black citizens continued to try to register as voters following Freedom Day, but few succeeded. Throughout the remainder of the year and in the first half of 1964, voting rights workers did not mount a campaign of organized resistance against the white power structure in Selma despite the psychological victory achieved in the fall of 1963. Rather, they focused on holding mass meetings and citizenship classes. However, on July 5, three days after the enactment of the Civil Rights Act of 1964, voting rights workers staged a registration rally in downtown Selma. Sheriff Clark's deputies and members of an unofficial posse wielded nightsticks and tear gas to quickly suppress the demonstration. The following day, SNCC chair John Lewis led a voter registration march on the county courthouse. Clark confronted the marchers personally and attempted to bully them into leaving, but Lewis responded, "We are going to stay here until these people are allowed to register and vote."[7] Law enforcement officials led the demonstrators into an alley, arrested fifty, and seared several with electric cattle prods as they marched the protestors five blocks to the county jail. Saddled by the intimidation, obstruction, and retaliation operation headed by Clark—and a July 9 injunction that prohibited any "assembly of three persons or more in a public place" sponsored by civil rights organizations—the voting rights campaign in Selma went underground and nearly came to a halt.

Throughout the struggle in Selma, the Justice Department initiated court cases to help black residents there gain access to the ballot box, but litigation proceeded at a snail's pace, and the department's efforts often failed. In 1963 the Justice Department charged Selma officials with intimidating prospective African American voters by assaulting and arresting voting rights workers on baseless charges (*United States v. Dallas County*), sought to enjoin misuse of the state law enforcement machinery to intimidate local blacks for the purpose of interfering with their right to vote (*United States v. McLeod*), charged that the local citizens' council used threats and intimidation to interfere with African Americans' right to vote and intended to frustrate federal court orders (*United States v. Dallas County Citizens Council*), and accused city and county officials of interfering with black citizens' right to vote (*United States v. Clark*).[8] Nevertheless, Federal District Court judge

Daniel Thomas—a segregationist determined to bar blacks from casting ballots—delayed hearings and then issued his often unfavorable rulings long after hearing the cases. Though the Justice Department achieved minor victories by appealing Thomas's rulings to the Fifth Circuit Court of Appeals, including an injunction against the Dallas County registrars in November 1963, the judge's tactics of delay helped keep the mechanisms of voter discrimination running in Selma into the spring of 1965.

Selma: Escalation

Determined to jump-start a campaign stalled by local oppression and court delays, Selma voting rights activists contacted Martin Luther King Jr. in October 1964 and urged him to help their cause. King's Southern Christian Leadership Conference (SCLC) had initially planned to help organize the Selma campaign but focused instead on a desegregation campaign in Saint Augustine, Florida. However, the request for assistance from Selma coincided with the SCLC's new plans to initiate a statewide voting rights crusade in Alabama. Voting had become a primary focus of the civil rights movement following the passage of the Civil Rights Act of 1964, and King hoped to attain a national victory on voting rights analogous to that for desegregation achieved by the Birmingham protests. SCLC director of direct action James Bevel was already canvassing Alabama as part of a grassroots voter registration project, and he urged his colleagues to focus the organization's energies in "the heart of Dixie." During its staff retreat in Birmingham on November 10–12, the SCLC decided to launch its campaign in Selma after listening to Amelia Boynton's plea for support. The staff assigned Eric Kindberg to research the voting rights situation in Selma, C. T. Vivian to meet with local black leaders, and Bevel to plan direct action throughout Alabama. They also decided to begin the effort with a mass meeting featuring King on January 2, 1965, in defiance of State Circuit Court judge James Hare's order barring gatherings of three or more people.[9]

Even though Selma did not meet some of the SCLC's preferences for a direct action campaign—it was a small, isolated community, for example—the persistence, courage, determination, and defiant attitude of the town's black leadership made it an attractive locale. In addition, the SCLC believed that it could provoke Selma's unreasonable and intransigent law enforcement officials—especially Sheriff Clark—into lashing out and thus call attention to racist violence, as it had in Birmingham with Eugene "Bull" Connor. SCLC organizer Andrew Young understood that if Clark beat protestors "in front of CBS, NBC, and ABC television cameras," it would help create a televisual drama that would ultimately bring political change.[10] With their partnership in place, SCLC workers and local activists in Selma planned throughout November and December for the renewal of the voting rights campaign there at the start of the new year.

Upon King's involvement in the Selma campaign, the activism there took on broader political significance and became poised to become a symbol of the nationwide struggle by African Americans to register and vote. While King hoped to achieve a victory locally, he also hoped to help bring about a federal legislative solution to the problem of voter discrimination through the Selma campaign. Thus, King's activism in Selma thrust the local movement into the realm of national politics. In conversations with President Johnson in December and January, King did not discuss the Selma campaign specifically but emphasized the need for new voting rights legislation. Although Johnson seemed pessimistic about Congress's desire to pass a new civil rights bill in its current session, he shared King's belief that equal access to the franchise was a crucial next step in the struggle for racial justice. In a January 15 telephone conversation, the president told King that he believed a voting rights act was more important than the Civil Rights Act of 1964 and was a priority for his elected term as president. He also urged King, working in concert with other civil rights leaders, to publicize the worst instances of voting injustices in order to garner public support for electoral change—thus implicitly endorsing the Selma protests. Johnson claimed that, if the public were to see a dramatic example of the voter discrimination and intimidation practiced in the South, citizens would demand political action to set things right and make the electoral system fair.[11]

Selma was indeed home to some of the worst instances of voter discrimination and intimidation. Between 1954 and 1959, the local board of registrars registered only two of the approximately eight hundred applications filed by African American citizens. One qualified African American man applied thirty times yet was not registered. Between 1959 and 1961, the number of registered black voters in Dallas County fell from 163 to 156, or one percent of the black voting-age population; in contrast, sixty-four percent of whites in the county were registered voters. Between 1962 and 1963 the county board of registrars rejected nearly ninety percent of African American voter applicants. In 1964 a new statewide voter application form, which included a complicated literacy and knowledge test, made it even more difficult for blacks to register. The Dallas County registrars added a test not mandated by the new state law, requiring applicants to give a satisfactory (as determined by the local registrar) interpretation of an excerpt from the Constitution. The subjective nature of these tests permitted registrars, by design, to apply them in a racially discriminatory manner. In addition to facing the barriers erected by the registrars, potential black voters also faced intense, systematic intimidation from law enforcement officials and local whites, especially members of the Citizens' Council, including harassment, threats of economic or physical reprisal, baseless arrests, and physical violence.[12]

Selma was one of the worst cities for African Americans to try to register in as voters: In 1965 only 383 African Americans—less than two percent of the eligible black population—in Dallas County were registered voters. Perhaps some cities in Mississippi were worse than Selma, but even the Magnolia State as a whole, which many voting rights workers had abandoned as hopeless, had registered nearly seven percent of its eligible black citizenry.[13]

In 1965 the renewal of the voting rights campaign in Selma was a mixture of nuts-and-bolts registration efforts and measures designed to attract public attention. The SCLC expected that the inaugural mass meeting on January 2 would result in massive arrests—inside a church, Brown Chapel AME, no less. But Selma's new public safety director, Wilson Baker, announced that he would not enforce Judge Hare's ban

on assemblies; he hoped that, by using tactics that effectively countered SCLC's methods and defused publicity (like those employed by
Albany, Georgia, police chief Laurie Pritchett), he could calmly defeat
the voting rights campaign and usher the SCLC out of town.[14] Set-
tling into the business of attempting to register black citizens, voting
rights workers soon compiled maps of voting-age African American
households, canvassed those areas, elected block captains, held voter
education workshops, and resumed mass meetings. Yet the activists
still planned to organize events that would dramatize the plight of the
black residents who wanted to vote.

After some initial dithering, the public drama in Selma intensified at
the end of January. On January 18 civil rights workers and local citizens
marched on the Dallas County courthouse in the hope of registering
black voters and dramatizing voter discrimination in Selma. Both expectations went unfulfilled. Martin Luther King and John Lewis led a
phalanx of four hundred marchers to the courthouse. Law enforcement
officials promptly led them into an alley, out of journalists' view, where
they waited without anyone being invited to register. At that evening's
staff meeting, SCLC leaders decided that, if the next march proceeded
without incident, they would leave Selma for a nearby community more
amenable to its protest methods—either Marion, in Perry County, or
Camden, in Wilcox County.[15]

However, the events that unfolded in subsequent days convinced
the SCLC leaders to stay put in Selma. When marchers refused to be
shuffled into the alley the following day, Jim Clark grabbed one of them,
Amelia Boynton, in full view of reporters and "pushed her roughly and
swiftly for half a block into a patrol car." On January 23 Judge Thomas
issued an order that prohibited local officials from interfering with
voting registration efforts, but Clark quickly violated it. On January 25
the sheriff again assaulted marchers assembled in front of the courthouse. When Annie Lee Cooper—a fifty-three-year-old motel clerk
from Selma—met Clark's intimidation tactics by exclaiming, "Ain't
nobody scared around here," the sheriff pushed her, causing her to lose
her balance. After she regained her footing, Cooper punched Clark in
the left eye, knocking him to his knees. After Clark's deputies wrestled

Cooper to the ground, the sheriff "brought his billyclub down on her head with a whacking sound that was heard throughout the crowd gathered in the street." Clark's violent outbursts garnered national exposure for the Selma campaign: Newspapers published accounts and photographs of Clark's assault on Boynton and Cooper, which helped create the visual drama that civil rights organizers hoped would result in political change.[16] Although the board of registrars did not register any African Americans during the last two weeks of January, the arrest of hundreds of blacks in Selma and the attention brought about by Sheriff Clark's violent outbursts rejuvenated the voting rights campaign locally. James Bevel told the activists in Selma that the right to vote should be won by the end of the year.

In the beginning of February, activists encountered further violence and massive arrests but did not succeed in expanding the black electorate or creating an overwhelming exigency for an immediate legislative solution to the problem of black disfranchisement. On the first of the month, King led a column of several hundred marchers out of Brown Chapel. They advanced in a single group—in violation of the city's parade ordinance—in order to guarantee King's arrest, which movement leaders had deemed necessary to give the Selma campaign a publicity boost. Wilson Baker halted the group within a few blocks, and his officers arrested 270 marchers when they refused to disperse. Later in the day Sheriff Clark arrested an additional 500 marchers, most of them children.[17]

King refused bail until February 5, by which date local law enforcement officials had arrested more than one thousand voting rights activists. While in jail, King penned a public letter in which he observed that "there are more Negroes in jail with me than there are on the voting rolls" and described the methods of voter discrimination in Selma; the letter appeared as an advertisement in the New York Times on the day King posted bail. While activists waited to see whether the recent wave of arrests would focus attention on Selma, they learned of a judicial development that seemed poised to help their cause. On February 4 Judge Thomas ordered Dallas County's board of registrars to stop using Alabama's knowledge test, to discontinue rejecting voter applications because of minor errors, and to process at least one hundred voter applicants on each registration day. Though these developments were significant locally, some observers began to question whether the Selma campaign had the capability "to become another Birmingham"—to gain significant national attention. Furthermore, in a staff meeting on February 10, SCLC and SNCC officials claimed that the campaign had reached "a state of fatigue" and suggested planning for "some kind of victory" in Selma before moving the voting rights movement to Lowndes County, Alabama.[18]

The SCLC's voting rights campaign soon branched out into communities adjacent to Selma but still struggled to generate intense congressional and public outcry. Many newspapers and television news programs covered the events in Selma and surrounding communities during the beginning and middle of February, including a vicious attack on SCLC affiliates director C. T. Vivian by one of Clark's deputies on February 16. The campaign in Selma did—according to the *Congressional Quarterly Weekly Report*—give "fresh impetus" to "new legislation to assure Negroes the right to register and vote."[19] However, the pressure created by the Selma campaign in February was not strong enough to disrupt normal politics: Some members of Congress believed new legislation was needed, but legislators did not rally behind a single proposal or immediately take up the cause to pass a new voting rights law. In response to this failure, King stepped up the campaign on February 17 by urging more militant demonstrations and acts of civil disobedience, including nighttime marches.

The most violent and dramatic event in the SCLC-led campaign to date came on February 18 in Marion, a small town about twenty miles northwest of Selma. After a mass meeting in Marion that night, more than four hundred demonstrators marched out of Zion's Chapel Methodist Church and headed for the county jail to protest the arrest of voting rights organizer James Orange earlier in the day. After the marchers had gone less than half a block, a blockade of law enforcement officials, including state troopers dispatched by Alabama's public safety director, Col. Al Lingo, halted them. Police Chief T. O. Harris ordered the marchers to return to the church or disperse. When James

Dobynes, a minister and head of the march, kneeled to pray before retreating to the church, a state trooper struck him in the head with a club; two others then dragged him by the feet toward jail. Chaos and violence ensued. Law enforcement officials kicked, punched, clubbed, and whipped protestors as they ran for cover. They could not escape. The *New York Times* reported, "Negroes could be heard screaming, and loud whacks rang throughout the square." The marchers fled toward the church and into nearby buildings. Inside a café, state troopers attacked demonstrators, including an eighty-two-year-old man. When his daughter, Viola Jackson, tried to protect him, police knocked her to the floor. When her son, Jimmie Lee Jackson, lunged to protect her, one trooper threw him against a cigarette machine, and another shot him twice in the stomach. As Jackson buckled and bled, the two troopers beat and pushed him out of the café. Additional troopers struck Jackson as he stumbled toward the bus station, where he collapsed. Nearby marchers picked Jackson up and drove him to the county hospital; doctors soon transferred him to Good Samaritan Hospital in Selma. Jackson, a local resident who had applied to vote five times at the Perry County courthouse, died eight days later.[20]

The violence against marchers raised tensions in Dallas, Perry, and Wilcox counties. On February 19 SCLC head of voter registration Hosea Williams agreed to temporarily halt night marches in order to avoid further bloodshed. On February 20 Alabama governor George Wallace denounced and banned nighttime marchers in the Selma area. Two days later King suggested that voting rights workers organize a motorcade to drive disfranchised blacks to the state capitol in Montgomery to protest voter discrimination. That same evening Ross Barnett, a staunch segregationist and former governor of Mississippi, addressed a crowd of two thousand attending a Dallas County Citizens' Council rally. Following the assembly, a greater number of hostile whites gathered around the demonstrations in Selma. On February 23 King announced that a motorcade to the capitol was scheduled for March 8. The next few days were quiet in Selma, but soon after Jimmie Lee Jackson's death on February 26, James Bevel announced at a memorial service that the voting rights campaign would intensify. He also raised the idea of large numbers of disfranchised African Americans marching, not driving, the fifty-four miles to Montgomery to protest voter discrimination and honor Jackson's memory. Bevel's idea quickly gained currency among voting rights workers. As it became formalized in early March and as law enforcement officials and local whites planned their opposition to the demonstration, the campaign in Selma headed toward a decisive, dramatic confrontation.

Selma: Eruption

In the first week of March, the voting rights campaign in Selma heated up as protestors and law enforcement officials planned for the march to Montgomery. On the first of the month, King led rallying marches in Dallas, Wilcox, and Lowndes counties. At the assembly in Selma, he expressed his confidence that the campaign would soon achieve its largest goal: "We are going to bring a voting rights bill into being in the streets of Selma." On March 3 Bevel announced to the press that the march to the capitol would take place on Sunday, March 7, with King leading the procession. The following day, Governor Wallace met with his advisers and state public safety officers to discuss how to manage the march. They planned to encourage the demonstrators to halt but let them proceed if force were necessary to stop them. The group also planned to then cut off supply lines and restrict media access to Highway 80 between Selma and Montgomery, believing this would stifle the march. On March 5 King traveled to the nation's capital to meet with President Johnson, who said he would soon introduce a voting rights bill to Congress and believed its prospect for passage was good.[21]

Johnson's message of support and optimism was good news, but the activists still needed to solidify public opinion behind prompt enactment of a strong federal voting rights statute. While King met with the nation's chief executive, Alabama's executive decided to block the Selma march, now believing that local whites would commit violence against the demonstrators, thus creating a public debacle. Wallace met with Colonel Lingo and his deputies and agreed to allow law enforcement officials to halt the marchers and turn them around, using the minimum amount of force necessary. On March 6 the governor issued a formal statement banning the march, which he claimed would threaten public safety, interrupt traffic, and disrupt commerce. In Selma, Wilson Baker surmised correctly that Al Lingo and Jim Clark were clandestinely making plans to stop the march with violence, despite assurances to the contrary and Clark's departure for the weekend.

Aware of the possibility—though not inevitability—of violence, the marchers prepared themselves physically, mentally, and spiritually for the fifty-four-mile trek. Absent from the preparations, however, were most SNCC workers; the committee refused to endorse a march it believed was doomed to encounter violence and drain resources and energy from the campaign. Even more surprising than SNCC's official repudiation was King's decision on the eve of the demonstration to remain in Atlanta rather than return to Selma to lead the procession. Fearing that the recent, credible threats to murder King would be carried out, Hosea Williams and Jim Bevel suggested that King stay in Atlanta. King suggested deferring the march until Monday, hoping that federal district court judge Frank Johnson Jr. would void the governor's ban, but Williams and Bevel said that local enthusiasm for the march demanded that it not be postponed. Believing that law enforcement officials would only arrest the marchers—and feeling bound to honor his commitment to preach at Ebenezer Baptist Church on Sunday rather than spend more time in the Dallas County jail—King decided to remain in Atlanta.[22]

Late into the morning of Sunday, March 7, questions remained about whether the marchers would proceed as planned and, if so, how far they were likely to travel. Wishing that King were there to lead them, some of the activists were hesitant about going ahead only to encounter the troopers now waiting for them. To settle the issue, Williams telephoned King's church in Atlanta. Reluctantly, King ruled that the march should continue as planned. He directed SCLC leaders Bevel, Williams, and Andrew Young to choose one among their number to lead the demonstrators with John Lewis (who was marching without the official support of SNCC) while the other two men stayed behind to manage contingencies. By a coin toss, Williams was designated at the march's co-leader. Although the activists were now ready to set out, they did not expect to actually reach Montgomery but rather to be turned around by the law enforcement officials blocking Highway 80. If the officers allowed the demonstrators to pass, the march would become an ad hoc protest since many of the participants were still dressed in their Sunday best and unprepared for a fifty-four-mile trek to the state capitol.

Around 4 P.M. Lewis read a short statement for the press; Young delivered a brief prayer; and the six hundred marchers set out from Brown Chapel, double file, uncertain about how events would unfold. The protestors walked along Sylvan, Water, and Broad streets and then reached the Edmund Pettus Bridge, which spans the Alabama River. As they approached the bridge's apex, they could see state troopers spread shoulder to shoulder across the highway and a group of Clark's posse, most on horseback, stationed behind the troopers. A large crowd of hostile whites, a small group of African Americans, and a cadre of journalists had gathered on the side of the road. Jim Clark, who had just returned to Selma, and Al Lingo sat in an unmarked car parked roadside. When the marchers came within fifty feet of the troopers, Maj. John Cloud—the officer in charge—ordered them to stop. Using a bull horn, he called out, "This march will not continue." The marchers halted. Cloud then announced, "This is an unlawful assembly. This demonstration will not continue. You are ordered to disperse and go back to your church or to your homes." Williams asked to speak with Cloud, but the major replied, "No, I will give you two minutes to leave." The marchers did not move. Williams and Lewis decided to spread the word that the marchers should kneel and pray. However, just one minute after issuing his two-minute warning and before most of the marchers had knelt, Cloud astonished them by issuing an attack order: "Troopers, advance!"[23]

The troopers and members of the posse rushed forward to assault the marchers. The officers clubbed them, flailed them with bullwhips, and seared them with electric cattle prods. The attack sent many of the protestors to the ground and those still standing into a lumbering retreat. The horsemen from Clark's posse then charged full speed into the withdrawing mass of demonstrators. Troopers fired tear gas canisters into the crowd. Local whites cheered the lawmen on, exclaiming, "Get the niggers!" Helpless men, women, and children became incapacitated and lay strewn across the bridge—bleeding, weeping, and vomiting. Troopers blocked ambulances that were trying to cross the bridge to reach the wounded. As the marchers eventually began to escape the attack site, their assailants—which now included Clark—chased them back into the neighborhood surrounding Brown Chapel. Violence continued. The lawmen beat the marchers remaining on the street, fired teargas into the nearby First Baptist Church, and threw a black teenager through a window. Wilson Baker soon arrived on the scene and eventually restrained Clark's posse and the state troopers from further assaults.[24]

Injuries to the marchers were severe. They sustained fractured ribs and arms, severe head gashes, and broken teeth, in addition to more minor injuries received from the beatings and tear gas attack. John Lewis's skull was fractured by a state trooper's blow. Another officer knocked Amelia Boynton unconscious. Ambulances transported the injured to Good Samaritan Hospital and the Burwell Infirmary.

When the situation in Selma subsided, the campaign leaders attempted to calm and reassure the marchers and plotted their next steps. Williams and Lewis led a mass meeting in Brown Chapel, which was followed by an SCLC strategy meeting. Williams and Young telephoned King, who was horrified by the news. King announced that the SCLC should encourage supporters to deluge the White House and the capitol with telegrams deploring the violence and urge civil rights supporters to converge on Selma for a second march to Montgomery on Tuesday. King planned to have attorneys seek a federal injunction to prevent interference with the march and to send telegrams to religious leaders asking them to participate.

Selma: Denouement

Soon after the state troopers and the posse attacked the marchers, journalists disseminated images and accounts of the brutality and bloodshed. Although Clark thought he had pushed the photojournalists and TV cameras back far enough from the action for them to be unable to get good pictures, they nevertheless captured vivid images of the massacre.[25] Around 9:00 P.M. ABC TV interrupted its evening movie with a special news bulletin: Anchor Frank Reynolds told viewers about the brutal clash and then cut to fifteen minutes of footage from the assault at Pettus Bridge. On Monday morning, the front pages of major newspapers were emblazoned with headlines about the assault. The accompanying photographs showed graphic scenes of troopers and mounted posse beating protesters with nightsticks. The visual drama made the discrimination and harassment in Selma seem more real and more critical. Writers soon dubbed the day "Bloody Sunday."

Americans responded with alarm and outrage to what they heard, read, and saw in the news. Citizens and editorialists called the events "shameful" and "a disgrace." The *Christian Science Monitor* reported that the nation experienced "widespread shock" upon learning of the violence against the peaceful marchers and that the "conscience of the nation and the world has been outraged by the brutal tactics of Governor Wallace's state troopers." The *Monitor* also reported that citizens were "profoundly horrified at the events in Alabama" and that no event in the civil rights movement had "made a deeper and more poignant impression on American public opinion than the beatings and proddings and bull whippings." Thousands of Americans expressed their anger at the violence in Selma by participating in protests nationwide: Citizens staged sympathy marches in Boston, Buffalo, Chicago, Cincinnati, Detroit, Hartford, Kansas City, Los Angeles, Madison, Milwaukee, New York, Philadelphia, San Francisco, Trenton, and Washington, D.C.[26]

The international community also responded with indignation to the violence in Selma. Most of the foreign press waited to see how the U.S. government would respond and then lauded Washington for its commitment to racial justice, but the *Manchester Guardian* expressed a sentiment shared privately among many international citizens and leaders, calling Sunday's attack "a major blemish on the face of American society." Several nations criticized the United States more strongly. In the Soviet Union, the media claimed that the assault effectively revealed "America's shame," the oppression of its own people. The Vietnamese daily *Trung Lap* also condemned the attack and claimed that the Selma situation exposed Americans as hypocritical since the United States sought to export "democracy and liberty to underdeveloped countries" while oppressing and disfranchising its own citizens.[27]

The nation's wrath was exacerbated by events that unfolded in the days after the "Bloody Sunday" attack. More than 1,500 citizens, including about 450 members of the clergy, responded to King's call to participate in a second march attempt on Tuesday, March 9. Unknown to the rank-and-file marchers, King agreed to a deal brokered by White House liaison LeRoy Collins, which permitted the demonstrators to make a symbolic statement but avoid arrest for violating a federal court injunction against the march and avert another violent encounter with Alabama state troopers. Around 2:30 P.M. on Tuesday, 3,000 marchers headed out from Brown Chapel, aimed toward Montgomery. After the columns were again halted by Major Cloud, though, King turned the marchers around and led the procession back to its starting point, to the astonishment—and in some cases anger—of those involved. Though the short, controversial march was peaceful, local citizens disturbed the calm that evening. While dining, four local whites spotted a group of white ministers who had participated in the march. The men burst out of the café, shouting "Hey, you, niggers!" and then attacked the clergymen. One of the assailants struck Unitarian minister James Reeb in the head with a club or pipe. After two days of medical treatment for his severe head injury, Reeb died in a Birmingham hospital on Thursday evening, March 11. That white supremacists had murdered someone, especially a minister, for demonstrating solidarity with the voting rights workers in Selma increased the indignation of the American people.[28]

Although horrible, the bloodshed in Selma helped the SCLC achieve its goal of creating a public and congressional exigency that hastened the enactment of a new federal voting rights statute. Newspapers reported that the demonstrators had succeeded in "mobilizing formidable national sentiment behind new civil-rights legislation" and that the public opinion aroused by "Bloody Sunday" made it "inevitable that American citizens, whatever their color, will get the right to vote." News accounts also noted that "Congressional pressure for a new voting rights law mounted . . . as members of both parties expressed anger and disgust at Alabama's violent repression of the Negro marchers in Selma." The concern that many citizens and legislators had expressed just weeks earlier—that "Negroes were pushing too fast"—seemed to evaporate after the brutal attack at the Pettus Bridge.[29]

Conclusion

Lyndon Johnson soon found himself at the center of the political emergency brought about by the violence in Selma: Citizens and members of Congress turned to LBJ as the person who was expected to solve the crisis. People criticized him for not preventing the confrontation, for not responding to it effectively, and for not sending new voting rights legislation to Congress quickly enough. Reflecting on the situation in his memoirs, President Johnson stated, "Everywhere I looked I was being denounced for my 'unbelievable lack of action.'" Nearly everyone who denounced the events at Selma and what they perceived as presidential inaction also looked to Johnson for a decisive rhetorical response. He had spoken out about the violence in Selma and voting rights legislation, but critics argued that his previous statements were supportive but "not strong enough" and that he had not gone "as far as he should have."[30]

Johnson's "We Shall Overcome" speech, then, was not merely a reaction to the circumstances in Selma but rather became an integral part of the historical configuration anchored there. Americans expected LBJ to state clearly what the federal government would do to resolve the crisis, and I believe they also wanted him to condemn the violence on behalf of the nation, purge the country's guilt in that such atrocities had happened in the United States, and interpret the events in Selma and the nation's response in a way that gave them deep meaning.

President Johnson met these rhetorical expectations creatively by relating the events in Selma to America's political creeds and commitments. He did not denounce the violence personally or emotionally; rather, he deplored it philosophically, criticizing the state troopers in Selma for resorting to "the force of arms and tear gas" instead of upholding "law and order." The president asserted that the discrimination and violence in Selma had tarnished national dignity and pride yet suggested that the United States could reestablish them by recommitting itself "to the values and the purposes and the meaning of our beloved nation." Rather than focusing Americans' attention inward on the immediate historical moment, Johnson focused it outward onto a broader historical landscape, in which current events took on their meaning by how they related to the nation's realization of its commitments to equality and justice. In short, Johnson transformed himself from an observer of and respondent to the Selma protests into a participant in the political crisis they triggered. He took on the role of the prophet who identified the nation's sins and recalled its people to their original task.

Johnson's "We Shall Overcome" speech interpreted the events in Selma innovatively, argued effectively from the history of voter discrimination there and elsewhere to advocate legislation, and skillfully managed the public emotions elicited by the violence in Selma. Still, the speech had a few shortcomings in regard to its interaction with history. First, the president failed to discuss the extended history of voting rights activism, which would have reinforced the notion that both African American protest and Johnson's request for the immediate passage of a strong voting rights law were prudent and timely. Second, despite his praise for their courage, LBJ alienated some black activists by alluding to the murder of James Reeb (a white minister) as an atrocity of the voting rights campaign but omitting mention of the murder of Jimmie Lee Jackson (a black pulpwood worker). Third, Johnson failed to address a prominent public concern raised by the events in Selma—the need to extend federal protection to voting rights workers. He could have managed these historical events and concerns successfully in order to make his inventive, effective, skillful public appeal even stronger.

A final, arguable criticism of Johnson's rhetorical ability to meet historical demands and manage historical events is that the president should have spoken his words sooner. LBJ's speech did not come until eight days after "Bloody Sunday," and some observers at the time deemed it overdue, given the gravity and urgency of recent events. Though attentive to the feelings of crisis aroused by the Selma protests, President Johnson also believed that the status of the White House's legislative proposal should influence the timing of his message. Since he wanted a solid proposal in hand before addressing the Congress, a critique of his rhetorical timing must be informed by an understanding of the history of the administration's efforts to develop a new federal voting rights bill—the subject of the next chapter.

CHAPTER THREE

Plotting to Secure the Franchise

As a legislative leader, Lyndon Johnson possessed an acute concern with the future: He reflected on the persistence of political problems, thought through the long-term implications of policy proposals, and sought to predict how history would view his actions. But as a rhetorical leader, LBJ often seemed unable to work out the long-term consequences of his persuasive strategies. Critics often deride Johnson as a short-sighted communicator who tried to rally public support for his programs before he had fully developed them. Scholars note that he spoke prematurely, in language that aroused expectations beyond what he could achieve and without evaluating the possible impact of his communication on the policymaking process. Though some Americans felt that President Johnson responded too late to civil rights problems, including the situation in Selma, scholars suggest he regularly spoke too soon—before he had developed thorough policy responses to political crises.[1]

Nonetheless, the Selma situation was different. Careful study of the events preceding the president's "We Shall Overcome" speech show that LBJ prepared his legislative proposal before the crisis came and that his understanding of civil rights as a moral and legislative issue seemed to develop during this time. In 1964 and 1965 careful deliberations and detailed policy discussions of the voting rights bill preceded discussions of public rhetoric. In contrast to what most scholars would predict, the White House spent much more time developing a bill to secure equal voting rights rather than devising a campaign to pitch it to Congress and the public. In fact, the public, protesters, and legislators criticized Johnson for spending too much time formulating legislation and for not speaking soon enough in response to the violence at Selma.

President Johnson briefly discussed legislation to secure equal voting rights before March 15 but delayed a major speech on the issue until his administration had prepared a solid legislative proposal. He wanted to avoid constraining his legislative options, a possible consequence of speaking out before the Justice Department had settled on a particular approach to the problem of voter discrimination. LBJ wanted to reference the major provisions of a bill in his speech rather than present a broad outline, which would have failed to satisfy many civil rights activists and legislators. In order not to go over their heads, he wanted to consult with members of Congress about his legislative proposal before speaking. And he wanted to announce his legislative intention in a climate of relative calm to avoid the appearance that the White House had prepared legislation hastily.

By investigating the administrative history of the voting rights bill in more detail, we will see how the legislative process, in conjunction with the Selma protests, influenced the timing and strategy of President Johnson's "We Shall Overcome" speech. Though his address and the legislative process were appropriately pressured by the Selma demonstrations, the president also managed the public crisis created by the demonstrations to make a persuasive case for legislation that he had already planned to pursue but that only recently became available and possible. An effective response to the rhetorical situation as the president interpreted it, then, was connected to the dynamics of protest and legislation.

Planning

Lyndon Johnson expressed his desire to secure voting rights legislation long before the Selma crisis, beginning in 1963. According to White

House aide Jack Valenti, LBJ told his aides immediately after assuming the presidency in November that he planned to pass a voting rights measure separate from the bill that ultimately became the Civil Rights Act of 1964. A December memorandum from State Department official G. Mennen Williams to the president confirms that the Johnson administration was discussing voting rights in its earliest days. Also in December 1963, the President's Commission on Registration and Voting Participation suggested that the federal government act to end racial discrimination by voting to ensure that more U.S. citizens exercise the franchise.[2]

The administration's interest in a new voting rights statute did not become a more active pursuit, however, until the middle of 1964. That year, the White House created fourteen task forces to investigate political problems and, assuming LBJ were reelected, develop policy ideas to be pursued in 1965. On June 17 the civil rights task force finalized its issue paper, which listed voting rights legislation as a "minimum additional measure" needed to address the nation's persistent civil rights problems. The issue paper claimed that the administration could not focus merely on implementing the Civil Rights Act of 1964 and enforcing its provisions but rather must immediately make "strong moves to insure the speediest possible accession of Negroes to voting rolls, especially in the South."[3]

Immediately after the signing of the Civil Rights Act of 1964 on July 2, Johnson made it known within the administration that he planned to pursue a voting rights law, even though he did not establish a firm timetable for its introduction. According to Eric Goldman, special consultant to the president, LBJ instructed the Justice Department to prepare recommendations on how to help secure equal voting rights during this time. Goldman notes, however, that "the assignment was long-range" since the president wanted to give the nation time to digest the 1964 statute. Indeed, given the recent enactment of a new civil rights law, some White House aides urged the president to wait until 1966 to pursue a new voting rights measure. Several historians, including Goldman and former White House fellow Doris Kearns Goodwin, have concluded that LBJ did not intend to push for the legislation in

1965 but was forced into action by the Selma campaign. This contention is mistaken. President Johnson did have doubts about whether
he could persuade Congress to pass a new civil rights law in 1965, but
he planned to move forward with proposals and legislative drafting
despite his concern. His chief legislative liaison, Lawrence O'Brien,
claims, "There was never any indication given to me by Johnson of
any planned delay on voting rights. It was coming right after the 1964
Act.... He was hell-bent to get every piece of civil rights legislation he
could get."[4] Archival materials at the Johnson presidential library also
reveal that the White House's planning for voting rights legislation
intensified before Martin Luther King Jr. stepped up the campaign in
Selma, especially in December. LBJ believed that the only way to help
African Americans achieve political equality was "through the ballot
box," and his commitment to equal voting rights seemed to intensify
in 1964.[5]

Factors in addition to the president's commitment to equal rights
may have nudged the administration into pursuing a voting rights bill.
In November 1964 Johnson confidant Louis Martin urged the Democratic Party to pursue African American voters to compensate for the
loss of white votes in the South due to the administration's civil rights
policies. To achieve this goal, Martin urged party officials to promote
black voter registration and elected Democrats to help pass a new voter
rights measure. In December, Matthew Reese, the Democratic National Committee's director of operations, circulated a memorandum
throughout the party and the White House urging immediate legislative
reform to end the "antiquated election laws and practices which actually obstruct the path to the ballot box." Though the memo justified
voting rights legislation in terms of democratic principles, its subtext
is that such legislation would help enfranchise citizens who would cast
their ballots for Democratic candidates. Historian John Andrew's claim
that "party politics, perhaps more than civil rights, called the shots"
on voting rights policy overstates the case, but President Johnson and
his advisers certainly understood that some political advantage might
come from enacting legislation that would guarantee equal access to
the franchise.[6]

Preliminary Drafting

By December, White House officials were working fervently to develop a voting rights proposal. On December 18 President Johnson emphasized his commitment to legislation in a telephone conversation with Attorney General Nicholas Katzenbach, entreating him to use the best talent in the Justice Department to develop "a simple, effective method" to guarantee African American voter registration. LBJ also stressed urgency, directing Katzenbach "to undertake the greatest midnight legislative drafting" session and encouraging him to complete a proposal within the next few days so that it would be ready for the 1965 legislative program. The president also told the attorney general that, if legislation to end disfranchisement was likely to be ineffective or ruled unconstitutional, Katzenbach should draft a constitutional amendment to solve the problem. Ten days later, Harold Greene, an attorney in the Justice Department's Civil Rights Division, presented an overview of three voting rights proposals to the attorney general, who endorsed it and forwarded the recommendations to President Johnson. Greene outlined three approaches to solving the voting rights problem, which he ranked in descending order of preference: (1) a constitutional amendment prohibiting the states from imposing voter qualification on any basis other than age, residency, criminal record, or psychiatric institutionalization; (2) legislation investing a federal commission with the power to conduct registration for federal elections; or (3) legislation granting a federal agency the power to assume direct control of registration in both federal and state elections in any area where the percentage of potential African American votes was low.[7]

Whereas the Justice Department favored a constitutional amendment, the president and his advisers initially endorsed Greene's second proposal—legislation authorizing the use of federal voting registrars—but kept their minds open to alternatives. As Johnson and his aides developed the State of the Union address, they decided that the president should announce at that time his intention to recommend voting rights legislation to Congress in 1965. Some of the presidential advisers questioned this decision. In a December 30, 1964, memorandum to White House chief of staff Bill Moyers, special council Lee White wrote, "Certainly I have no problem with the desirability of such legislation, but I do have a problem about the timing." White urged that the president not propose legislation now but instead "call attention to the importance of registration and indicate that 1965 was to be a year of test," in which substantial progress must come in order to forestall federal intervention, to be proscribed by voting rights legislation introduced in 1966. LBJ continued to confer with the Justice Department, however, and had firmly made up his mind to pursue a legislative solution to the problem of voter discrimination nearly a week before King began to reinvigorate the Selma voting rights campaign.[8]

During the first month of the new year, the Johnson administration stepped up its pursuit of the legislation, publicly announcing its intentions and beginning the process of drafting specific measures to address voter discrimination. In a press conference just prior to the president's January 4, 1965, State of the Union address, Bill Moyers announced that LBJ would "make proposals to deal with the arbitrary restrictions to the exercise of the vote" but pointed out that "whether these will take the form of a constitutional amendment or legislation has not been decided." In the State of the Union message, the president urged Congress to "eliminate every remaining obstacle to the right and opportunity to vote" and announced that within six weeks he would send a detailed proposal on voting rights to Congress. After the speech, the *Washington Post* reported that passage of a constitutional amendment or legislation "may require all the persuasion the President can muster." Before mustering persuasion, however, the White House assembled its troops and dispatched them to draft voting rights measures post haste. On January 8 the Justice Department completed a draft of a constitutional amendment, and three days later the attorney general informed LBJ that Civil Rights Division attorneys were drafting a bill "to implement the President's State of the Union Message remarks with respect to the elimination of barriers to the right to vote." On January 18, the day of the first SCLC-led march on the Dallas County Courthouse, the attorney general informed LBJ that he planned to have a first draft of a bill ready on January 25 or 26 and that Justice Department officials were also preparing a written message to Congress to accompany the legislation.[9]

Drafting a bill took longer than Katzenbach had predicted, and as the White House waited for a draft, other political actors became involved in the process. On February 2 King requested a congressional investigation of voting conditions in Alabama, and three days later an unofficial delegation of fifteen House Democrats and Republicans visited Selma to observe its methods of voter registration. On February 8 two voting rights proposals were introduced in the House, but most of the representatives seemed willing to wait for a proposal from the White House. On February 10 eleven of the congressmen who visited Selma sent a telegram to Johnson that urged immediate action. Despite their position as legislators, the congressmen suggested the president assume control of the legislative process: "It is the consensus of our group that further legislation is necessary to insure the right to vote of these and all citizens. . . . We respectfully urge these proposals be enacted this year, and we specifically suggest that such legislation include a provision for a system of voter registration by federal authorities." Lee White replied to the telegram, recommending that the legislators meet with attorneys in the Justice Department's Civil Rights Division to discuss specific legislative recommendations. During this waiting period, President Johnson announced that he intended to see the right to vote "secured for all of our citizens" and disclosed that he would send a voting rights bill and an accompanying message to Congress "very soon."[10]

In mid-February, administration officials focused on a legislative approach to ending literacy and comprehension tests instead of a constitutional amendment, which had been advocated by some administration officials and several civil rights leaders. White House officials came to believe that a constitutional amendment would be less effective and take too long to enact. In a February 15 memorandum, Deputy Attorney General Ramsey Clark noted that, after consultation with legislators, civil rights leaders, census bureau officials, and other advisers, the Justice Department had decided that "a constitutional amendment would not be a satisfactory approach." Clark noted that

Justice Department attorneys would soon complete a draft of the proposed legislation.[11]

Under Pressure

Despite frequent suggestions that the Justice Department would draft a bill quickly, the actual process moved slowly. The chief legal problem was developing a straightforward method for measuring racial discrimination in voting—which was not a straightforward practice—and determining when federal registrars would assume control of local elections. Some Justice Department attorneys still believed this could be accomplished only by constitutional amendment, not statute, in view of the fact that the Constitution did not give the federal government any mechanism other than amendment to establish a national conception of voting rights. Others believed the department could draft an effective, constitutional voting rights law based on the Fifteenth Amendment. While officials struggled to overcome the practical and constitutional problems associated with voting rights legislation, the president prodded them to complete a draft promptly. Ramsey Clark stated that, before the Selma campaign created significant public pressure for legislative action, Johnson had pressured Justice Department officials to come up with a formula for determining racial discrimination in voting and for assigning federal registrars to solve the problem.[12]

Members of Congress also began to pressure the Justice Department and the president. On February 15 journalists Rowland Evans and Robert Novak reported that the Senate's civil rights bloc, which included a number of liberal Republicans, had demanded legislative details during a private conference with Attorney General Katzenbach and "an immediate push for a bill," a demand they renewed publicly less than two weeks later. On February 23 thirty-one Republicans prodded the White House to provide the details of its planned voting legislation and to send it to Congress immediately. Administration officials replied that the president would introduce a bill to the legislature "in a few days." However, the Justice Department only that day had completed a draft of a title outlawing the use of discriminatory "tests and devices" and would not have a draft of the provision on federal registrars ready for another few days. The department had formulated a legislative approach at this time (which is outlined in a draft of a written message to accompany the legislation, finished on February 24), but only two of the bill's anticipated three titles were written. Still, White House press secretary George Reedy announced on February 25 that he believed a bill would be sent to Capitol Hill within a few days, an optimism shared by some White House officials.[13]

On March 5, two days before the planned march from Selma to Montgomery, the Justice Department completed a draft of a federal voting rights bill. The White House kept this event private and still avoided disclosing the provisions of the legislation, as evidenced by LBJ's silence on the matter during his meeting with King on March 5. The administration remained silent, in part, because officials planned to solicit feedback from the Republican congressional leadership and incorporate its suggestions into a revised bill—a plan that would be undermined and/or complicated by publicly announcing the terms of the legislation. In addition, the White House remained quiet in order to avoid a public debate about the details with civil rights leaders, many of whom had advocated specific measures. King had announced five provisions he believed a new voting rights law should include; NAACP executive secretary Roy Wilkins had told the Senate Rules Committee that new legislation must provide for federal registrars; and the Mississippi Freedom Democratic Party (MFDP) had announced opposition to a bill that provided for federal registrars only if a certain level of voter registration had not been achieved and that applied only to hard-core areas of voter discrimination. The draft of the bill completed on March 5 was similar, in general, to the approach advocated by civil rights organizations. Nevertheless, there were differences, especially with the terms advocated by the MFDP, which might spark a debate. For this reason, the White House decided to avoid "being too specific about the details of the draft."[14]

The brutal attack on civil rights demonstrators at the Pettus Bridge on March 7 created even more pressure for the White House to quickly submit voting rights legislation and to outline its features, but Johnson and administration officials moved forward deliberately. Although, as the *New York Times* reported, "Congressional pressure for a new voting rights law mounted . . . as members of both parties expressed anger and disgust at Alabama's violent repression of the Negro marchers in Selma," Reedy announced on March 8 that the introduction of legislation was "still down the road a ways." Moreover, the attorney general refused to discuss the details with journalists, stating that they had yet not been settled.[15]

In private, Katzenbach reported to White House officials that his attorneys were revising the bill and the accompanying written message in response to feedback from administration officials and congressional leaders but stated that this process would delay the introduction of legislation. President Johnson showed restraint during the exigency provoked by the violence in Selma. The moment seemed ripe for him to introduce legislation that he had already planned to steer to passage, thus meeting legislators' demands and quelling criticism from them, as well as activists and citizens. LBJ wanted to introduce a sturdy, effective bill and to pave the way for its passage more than he wanted to introduce one immediately. Thus, the administration proceeded carefully, strengthening the provisions and including members of Congress in this initial legislative process.

On March 8, as it revised the proposed statute, the Justice Department secured significant victories in two voting rights cases it had argued before the Supreme Court. In the case of *Louisiana v. United States,* the high court invalidated the state's literacy and understanding test. In *United States v. Mississippi,* the court ruled that "the Attorney General has power to bring suit against a State and its officials to protect the voting rights of Negroes." The upshot of the two rulings was that the Justice Department could likely eradicate through litigation a chief form of voter discrimination used in the South at that time and that it could prosecute voting rights cases on a statewide basis rather than county by county.[16] The Supreme Court's ruling in *Louisiana* gave the Justice Department precedent to suspend literacy tests in its voting rights bill, which must have reduced its attorneys' anxiety as they finished drafting legislation. However, the *Mississippi* decision opened a line of counterargument to the case for a new voting rights statute: Opponents could argue that the federal government could and should seek to secure equal voting rights through litigation, which would be less arduous and time consuming than in the past—two of the attorney general's chief complaints that led him to advocate federal legislation. Though the high court's rulings had little impact on the provisions of a new voting rights bill, as it addressed other deficiencies of the litigation approach and promised to proceed more quickly still, the White House needed to anticipate counterarguments as it prepared its rhetorical campaign, including the written message to accompany the bill.

At the end of the week preceding President Johnson's "We Shall Overcome" speech, the administration revised its draft legislation and began to consider issues of political and rhetorical strategy. Justice Department officials labored to develop a revision that addressed congressional leaders' concerns about the circumstances under which literacy tests would be suspended and under which federal registrars would be appointed. Katzenbach told LBJ on March 10, however, that he worried that some congressional leaders would attempt to water down the administration's bill. The president directed the attorney general to continue working with select congressional leaders but—perhaps concerned that legislative fine-tuning and negotiation would delay the introduction of a bill for too long—pondered sending a written message to Congress on March 11 in advance of the legislation, despite his written statement of March 9, which declared that a message to Congress would not come until the bill was complete. Johnson was worried about not having a strong message on voting rights available to members of Congress and the public. Even though he decided to delay sending a written message and urged Katzenbach to take his time revising the bill to ensure its constitutionality, LBJ observed that people urgently wanted "information, details, explanations, and justifications" regarding the measure. Though some citizens and legislators criticized the president for the delay caused by his legislative strategy, he received some public support: During a March 12 broadcast about the political exigency induced by the brutality against protestors in Selma, CBS News commentator Eric Sevareid observed that "legislation written in the heat of emotion usually is bad legislation." That same day, the Justice Department completed the major revision that addressed congressional leaders' concerns.[17]

During the weekend preceding Johnson's address on Monday, March 15, the Justice Department endeavored to finish its voting rights bill, while administration officials publicly discussed the legislation in the greatest level of detail thus far. On March 13, Justice Department attorneys mostly made changes in wording to the previous day's draft bill, but they also revised it to explain in more detail how citizens registered by federal officials would proceed if faced with further obstruction at the polls. On that same day, following his Oval Office meeting with Alabama governor George Wallace, President Johnson held a press conference. He opened with a statement—the first he had delivered in person since "Bloody Sunday"—calling the violence in Selma "an American tragedy" and declaring that he would soon "send to the Congress a request for legislation to carry out the [Fifteenth] Amendment of the Constitution." Johnson described the bill only in general terms but stated that it would provide for federal registrars. Following the president's responses to the journalists' questions, Attorney General Katzenbach delivered a fifteen-minute, off-the-record background briefing on the content of the bill. Johnson then noted that a voting rights message would go to Congress on Monday, March 15, but might not be accompanied by legislation. His hedging about the date for submitting legislation reflected the realities of the revision process: On March 14 Justice Department officials consulted further with congressional leaders and made additional changes to the bill's language.[18]

Indeed, the Justice Department failed to finalize the bill before Monday. Its attorneys made more changes to the language on March 15, even as the president prepared to address the nation and submit a written voting rights message to Congress. In addition to these minor modifications, Justice Department officials revised the statute to include a new provision that declared an immediate moratorium on new voter qualifications in any jurisdiction covered by the law's trigger formula. The attorney general made a few minor, last-minute changes on Tuesday in time for President Johnson to submit the bill to Congress the following morning, Wednesday, March 17, as he promised in his "We Shall Overcome" speech.

Conclusion

Popular myth holds that the voting rights demonstrations in Selma, Alabama, created overwhelming political pressure among legislators and citizens, which in turn forced President Johnson to introduce voting rights legislation and push for its passage. An alternative, better-informed way to view the history of the Voting Rights Act of 1965, however, is to see the protests—which Johnson had encouraged—as having cultivated support for a policy to which the president had already committed himself and his administration. The events in Selma created a more intense exigency than LBJ perhaps expected, which complicated the political context in which his Justice Department had to write a voting rights bill. Yet Johnson, though insistent, tried to give the attorney general adequate time to prepare an effective, constitutional statute. The president avoided public messages that would constrain legislative options or be perceived as going over Congress's head. Indeed, the president did not plan to deliver a public speech on voting rights until urged by some members of Congress, focusing instead on a written message to accompany the legislation. To be sure, LBJ was attuned to rhetorical concerns, especially as critics continued to deride his relative silence and perceived delay. But in the end, President Johnson delivered a major address and transmitted a written message to Congress only after the administration had settled on its legislative approach, even though both came before he submitted the bill.

By waiting to introduce the administration's bill, Johnson guaranteed a better statute, benefited from demands for legislation cultivated by the Selma demonstrations, paved the way for passage by including influential members of Congress in the drafting, and found an opportune moment to address the nation. Although approval of a voting rights measure seemed likely by the time of the president's March 15 speech, LBJ's address could still serve a vital political function by persuading

Congress to pass the measure expeditiously and without weakening it—and by making these actions seem prudent. In addition, President Johnson and his advisers believed that the public crisis following the violence in Selma possessed rhetorical qualities not connected to legislation and planned to address those, too. In the next chapter we investigate the rhetorical strategies behind Johnson's "We Shall Overcome" speech and its argument, structure, language, style, and values in order to better understand and evaluate the political, cultural, and moral leadership accomplished through his address.

CHAPTER FOUR

Planning the Address

Given the energy invested in finalizing the voting rights bill, the White House devoted relatively little time to President Johnson's finest public speech. To be sure, LBJ and his aides were attuned to the way that presidential messages and silences would shape the president's public image, the legislative process, and the public exigency brought about by the Selma protests. However, until the final days of the voting rights crisis, the president's aides focused on preparing brief statements to be delivered at press conferences—oftentimes by White House officials rather than the president himself—and a written message to Congress that would accompany the voting rights bill. Johnson did not settle on a rhetorical strategy of speaking before Congress and the nation until the last moment. Even then, he seemed ambivalent about speaking publicly, realizing that, although many citizens wanted him to speak out, a major address still carried risks. Moreover, several trusted advisers and members of Congress counseled against a public speech. Ultimately, though, LBJ decided that further silence was unsuitable and that a written message to Congress was insufficient to assuage the sentiments of outrage, disgust, and guilt that possessed the nation—and to help achieve his political goals.

Once President Johnson decided to address Congress and the nation, he largely turned the process of preparing the speech over to his aides. He made some changes to the draft and inserted a few passages of his own, including brief passages extemporized during its actual delivery, but the address was composed mostly by members of his staff. As the product of others' hands, Johnson's "We Shall Overcome" speech is not a text that transparently displays the president's mind at work but meshes with his rhetorical style and his ideology on the issue of racial justice.

Just as the decision to speak and the speechwriting process were complicated, so too was the timing of the speech. The issue of voter discrimination had occupied LBJ's mind for some time: Privately, he had been working on a political solution to the problem and had encouraged civil rights activists to dramatize it. Still, the intense nature of the crisis in Selma disrupted the normal sense of time and seemed to discombobulate even the president, despite months of legislative planning and weeks spent monitoring the situation in Dallas County. At the same time, the crisis seemed to refine and mature his thinking on the issue of voting rights, and Johnson also realized that he used the urgency of the moment to ensure the passage of comprehensive federal legislation. Yet the moment for rhetorical action also seemed too late to some Americans, who believed the president to be behind the times. To address this complex situation, President Johnson's address aims to reframe his listeners' very sense of the past, present, and future.

In this chapter we examine the political and rhetorical dimensions of the president's decision to speak, investigate the speechwriting process, and consider the crucial matter of the rhetorical timing of LBJ's voting rights address.

Whither Speech

President Johnson's initial plan to propose a federal voting rights bill involved only a written message to Congress. At the end of February, special assistant to the president Horace Busby began drafting the written communication (based on an earlier version prepared by Justice Department officials)—the only one being prepared—though the president began to wonder whether he should make his case for new legislation in writing or in person. However, by the second week of March, White House officials began to suggest that the president deliver a major speech, too. The strongest recommendation came from Vice President Hubert Humphrey, who on March 12 advised LBJ to deliver a televised address that reaffirmed citizens' right to petition for redress of grievances, urged them to uphold law and order, formally announced the voting rights bill, and asked citizens to demand that members of Congress pass the bill promptly. Humphrey urged Johnson to go before the nation immediately—on either March 13 or 14—even if the final details were not complete by that time.[1]

LBJ had ambivalent feelings about formally communicating his voting rights message to Congress. With good reason, presidents infrequently deliver special messages to the legislature in person to push for a specific bill: Such speeches are risky. Johnson knew that a public address would put his power and popularity on the line. He also understood that taking his case to the public, while also addressing the Congress, could backfire politically if legislators came to feel that he had gone over their heads to pressure them into action. Yet he wanted to reassure citizens that the federal government was taking quick, decisive action to guarantee African Americans' access to the ballot box, a message best communicated by the president—in person. Although communication scholar Halford Ryan claims that the president had already made his decision to speak before his meeting with congressional leaders on the evening of March 14—and was thus manipulating them to solicit an invitation to address the Congress—it seems more likely that Johnson possessed an earnest ambivalence about a public address and made up his mind during the meeting.[2]

This evening meeting in the Cabinet Room initially focused on legislative concerns but quickly turned into a discussion about rhetorical strategy. After President Johnson reviewed his efforts to guarantee the right to vote and congressional leaders proposed dates for introducing the voting rights bill, Speaker of the House John McCormack suggested that the president consider delivering an address to a joint session of Congress. Senate minority leader Everett Dirksen, however, opposed such a speech. He contended that LBJ should not circumvent Congress by making a public appeal and should not let it seem that protestors had forced the federal government into action. Ignoring Dirksen's claims, Johnson countered that the public did not know what the government was doing to solve the problem of voter discrimination and suggested that a speech would meet an important need by showing the American people that "we are doing everything we can to solve this." Vice President Humphrey agreed, claiming that the president should deliver a televised speech to articulate "what this government is doing." House majority leader Carl Albert also advocated a public address, maintaining that a speech would not be a sign of panic, as Dirksen suggested, but rather would calm the tense situation and restore the public's confidence. Johnson then asserted that he must make some kind of public statement, either a written message released to the news media, a televised statement addressed to the American people, or a speech before Congress. Legislators soon agreed that the president should address a joint session of the Congress the following evening, Monday, March 15, and then send the voting rights bill to Capitol Hill on Wednesday. They also decided to issue a public invitation to President Johnson to address a joint session, which would make it seem that he was not going over the heads of members of Congress by allowing the speech to be televised. The invitation was reported in newspapers on Monday morning, as was the president's plan to address Congress "on the bipartisan voting rights bill he [would] recommend for speedy enactment."[3]

The president's decision to give a speech was the product of careful political calculations. He believed that he "had to reassure the people" that the White House was acting quickly and decisively to solve the problem of voter discrimination and also that "this reassurance would not be provided by the cold words of a written message."[4] But Johnson wanted much more than to reassure and convince the public of his active commitment to voting rights, thus immediately relieving pressure on himself. Above all, he wanted Congress to pass the voting rights bill to strengthen U.S. democracy and to ensure his place in history.

Even though a public speech carried risks, Johnson believed it was the best rhetorical means to ensure passage of the White House proposal. He was confident that his speechwriters could craft a message that presented a compelling public and congressional appeal on behalf of federal voting rights legislation, one that would efface his strategy of focusing public pressure to leverage legislators' support and strongly identify him with the nation's definitive voting rights law.

Speechwriting

Unlike some presidents, Lyndon Johnson generally participated little in the drafting of his speeches, even ones as significant as the voting rights address. Although he claimed that, in this case, he "wanted to reach the American people in [his] own words," he instead followed his usual routine and turned the speechwriting process over to his aides, maintaining little contact with those who prepared the address.

Unfortunately, the procedure that produced the "We Shall Overcome" address cannot be chronicled in complete detail. The principals involved in preparing the text for delivery have provided conflicting accounts of its drafting, and the archives of the Lyndon B. Johnson Library do not yield a detailed record of the process. Some facts are certain, however. First, Richard Goodwin—special assistant to the president—wrote the primary draft, which comprises roughly two-thirds of the final wording. Second, the procedure was piecemeal and carried out in haste. Most of Goodwin's draft is typed on paper that produced two carbon copies, but several pages are typed on heavy paper without carbons. Moreover, there is no collected, unedited draft of the ten pages that Goodwin wrote in the public statements collection at the Johnson Library, which suggests that he handed off his rough copy to the editors a few pages at a time or perhaps page by page. Third, the editing was also done bit by bit and hurriedly. Some of the editorial revisions are handwritten on the original typed pages; others on the carbon copies; some on photocopies; and still others are typed on new sheets of paper. The archives at the Johnson Library contain multiple, incomplete, edited drafts—some with comments penned by one editor, others with comments by several editors—which suggests that several aides modified the speech as they received pages from Goodwin or from an editor who preceded him. Fourth, someone at the White House compiled the revisions into a single draft, which then—following yet another revision—became the text the president used at the podium in the House chamber. Fifth, Johnson deviated from this copy during his delivery, making changes to the phrasing and adding new passages in places. Sixth, although President Johnson contributed relatively little to the content of the speech, White House officials took great care to give the impression that LBJ had composed it himself. The morning after the address, Special Assistant to the President Jack Valenti sent a memorandum to all staff members, directing them to respond to all inquiries regarding authorship with a statement similar to the following: "The President wrote the speech. He talked out what he wanted to say—and as drafts were prepared in response to his dictation, the President personally edited and revised."[5] Making claims that go beyond establishing these basic facts quickly becomes a speculative activity, given the limited archival materials that chronicle the speech's production and the contradictory claims made by those involved.

Perhaps the most disputed issue surrounding the production of the address relates to the speechwriting assignment. Soon after his meeting with congressional leaders on the evening of March 14, President Johnson headed to his private quarters in the White House to discuss the speech with Jack Valenti, the presidential aide in charge of speechwriting assignments. Valenti asserts that, during the course of their talk, he and LBJ agreed to entrust the speech to Dick Goodwin, whom he regarded as difficult but "a near genius in his field." Valenti claims he then contacted Goodwin and directed him to prepare a speech that emphasized the importance of racial justice to American democracy, reviewed the history of voting and voter discrimination in the United States, identified the problems of current voting laws, and outlined what needed to be done to solve the problem of black voter disfranchisement.[6] In contrast, Goodwin asserts that Valenti first delegated the speechwriting duty to Horace Busby and then reassigned it the following morning after the president insisted that Goodwin draft the address. But Bill Moyers, from whom Goodwin claims to have learned of the reassignment, does not corroborate this assertion, claiming to have no knowledge that Valenti took the task away from Busby and gave it to Goodwin.

Busby's primary duty related to the Selma crisis, however, was not speechwriting but drafting a written voting rights message that would accompany the White House bill when the president formally sent it to the Congress. Beginning on February 28, he produced a total of five drafts. At some point after preparing the third revision, dated March 12, Busby adopted a different approach for the final two drafts (both of which are undated), one more focused on the Fifteenth Amendment than on the broader history of voting in the United States. After adopting this approach, he also prepared a text that appears to be a rough copy of a speech rather than a written message. It begins with a salutation more fitting for an address: "Mr. Vice President, Mr. Speaker, Members of the 89th Congress." In addition, it contains language that calls attention to the president's physical presence before a congressional audience: "It is the duty of that Oath and the strength of my own abiding convictions that bring me before you tonight," and "I come to advise the Congress that if the Constitution is to be protected and defended . . . action by us is necessary, and it is necessary now." Busby's speech draft is very different from the primary text drafted by Goodwin: It emphasizes the mandate of the Constitution, the practices that keep African Americans from exercising their constitutional right, and the damage these racist practices inflict on the image of the United States abroad. Unfortunately, there are no archival documents that reveal who directed Busby to prepare a speech draft, when he prepared it, who received it, or how it came to be rejected.[7]

At present, participants in the speechwriting discussions and process agree on only two facts: (1) At some moment, President Johnson decided that Goodwin should prepare a speech draft; and (2) Goodwin ultimately composed the primary draft. Horace Busby passed away in 2000, and other former White House aides who might have possessed insights have no recollections of the speechwriting assignment. Though the archival record suggests that Busby did indeed prepare a draft, it does not clarify the dispute concerning the details of the assignment.[8]

A second controversy surrounding the production of the "We Shall Overcome" speech relates to the sources of its content. In his memoirs, President Johnson claims that, during a meeting with his staff on the evening of March 14, he "described the general outline of what [he] wanted to say." Former White House aide Eric Goldman claims that in outlining his message that evening, the president went so far as to pin down the exact phrasing of certain ideas. In point of fact, though, LBJ did not meet with his staff "for several hours" that night, as Johnson and Goldman claim: The president's daily diary reveals that he met with Vice President Humphrey in the Oval Office; dined with aides Jack Valenti and Harry McPherson at his residence; and talked via the telephone with his daughter Lynda, journalist Alfred Friendly, personal physician George Burkley, and civil rights leaders Whitney Young, Roy Wilkins, and Martin Luther King Jr. Johnson likely discussed the speech in broad terms with Valenti during their working dinner, but his intimation that his speechwriters merely fleshed out and refined a message from the president himself is misleading. In stark contrast to LBJ's account, Dick Goodwin asserts that he received no specific instructions—only a suggestion from Johnson that perhaps he include a passage about the president's experience as a teacher in Cotulla, Texas—for drafting the speech. Because he regularly attended Oval Office discussions about civil rights and was involved in policy making, Goodwin claims, the president did not need to brief him about what to write. Indeed, Goodwin describes his task in personal terms—to use strong, moralistic language that reflected his own convictions to express the president's historical, constitutional, and legal objections to voter discrimination. That the final text expresses Johnson's ideals in Johnson's style, Goodwin maintains, is the result of his familiarity with the president's personal and political sentiments and his man-ner of expression, not the result of following specific instructions or reproducing exact phrasing.[9]

Despite Goodwin's claims that he wrote the voting rights speech without input from others, his draft likely borrowed ideas and phrasing from several external sources. The clearest indication that he borrowed material is that his description of the methods used to keep African Americans from voting in the South is nearly identical to three paragraphs in Horace Busby's version (which are also contained in his drafts of the written voting rights message, prepared before Goodwin began his speechwriting task). In addition, two core appeals in Goodwin's draft—that emancipating the slaves represented a promise yet to be fulfilled and that, should it fail to solve the problem of racial discrimination, the United States will lose its soul and forfeit its special purpose and mission—are also the core appeals of an address LBJ delivered in Gettysburg, Pennsylvania. This speech, given while Johnson served as vice president, was also written by Busby; Goodwin may have referred to its text while preparing his draft of the voting rights address.

Goodwin may also have borrowed from a draft penned by Jack Rosenthal, special assistant to the attorney general. Rosenthal asserts that Attorney General Nicholas Katzenbach instructed him to prepare a speech draft weeks before the tensions in Selma climaxed, hoping that the president would speak out. Rosenthal states that the final version of LBJ's address was much more detailed and eloquent than his draft, yet claims that some of the language from his version did find its way into the text spoken by the president. Neither the archives at the Johnson Library nor the Justice Department records at the National Archives contain a draft penned by Rosenthal, but President Johnson did send Rosenthal an autographed copy of the text, which he claims LBJ sent as an expression of gratitude for his minor contributions to the address. Rosenthal did have some experience writing for the president: Earlier he had drafted remarks for Johnson to use in responding to reporters' questions about the situation in Selma.[10]

Finally, Goodwin's draft borrows heavily from the president's remarks at a press conference on March 13, following his meeting at the White House with Alabama governor George Wallace. Many of the major appeals in the voting rights address are also articulated in this statement: that the events at Selma have larger meaning as part of "the unending search for American freedom," that voting rights constitute a moral issue, that to deny citizens their vote is "to deny democracy itself" and "the promise of America," that the White House's voting rights bill embodies "the heart and the purpose and the meaning of America itself," and that the advocates of voting rights labor under God's guidance. The authorship of these appeals, however, cannot be determined. The task of preparing the press conference statement was divided into two parts: Bill Moyers crafted the remarks describing the president's meeting with Wallace, and another aide (who is not identified on the extant draft) prepared the opening remarks about the events in Selma and the voting rights bill. This anonymous typed version containing the major appeals of the address received some minor revisions from Goodwin, either Jack Valenti or Harry McPherson, and at least one other presidential aide (unfortunately, not all of the handwriting can be conclusively identified). Though Goodwin likely wrote this statement from which the "We Shall Overcome" speech borrowed so heavily and still penciled in his own editorial comments, one cannot rule out the possibility that another White House official is the author of these ancestral appeals.[11]

Once Goodwin completed his draft, several of Johnson's aides edited the speech, altering its language, explication, definition, and argument. Handwriting analysis of the edited drafts reveals that White House press secretary Bill Moyers penned most of the handwritten changes and that Jack Valenti made a few minor modifications. Additional changes appear to have been written by two, perhaps three, additional editors, who cannot be clearly identified by comparing the handwritten changes to handwriting samples from White House officials. Analysis of these samples does reveal, however, that none of the changes came from the hand of Lyndon Johnson, which contradicts claims that both he and the first lady made that LBJ "penciled in changes and rewrote sections" of the original speech draft.[12]

Most of the changes to Goodwin's draft are minor alterations in language that improve the speech's economy of expression, accuracy, and eloquence. For instance, Moyers economized Goodwin's sentence "Beyond this great chamber of the people we serve, and who sent us here" by excising its final phrase. He made the speech's command to "allow men to register and vote whatever the color of their skin" more equitable by inserting the word "women." He made an introductory paragraph more eloquent by removing the hackneyed simile "like some giant trumpet" as an adverbial modifier in the speech's reflection that "the cries of pain, the hymns and protests of oppressed people" had summoned the nation into action. Other adjustments in language were more significant, effecting changes in the speech's appeals and definitions. For example, the edited text stated that the civil rights struggle was for all "Americans," not just "American Negroes," and substituted the word "national" for the word "federal," a charged term that might have triggered negative emotional responses among Southern listeners dedicated to states' rights.

Several outright additions to Goodwin's draft also altered the speech's explication and argument. For example, editors added the claim that to deny the vote to African Americans was "to dishonor those who gave their lives for freedom" to its argument about voting rights. Another addition emphasized that the United States' reputation was at stake in that outside the House chamber lurked "the grave concern of many nations" in addition to the conscience of the American people. Another editorial insertion described more clearly the objectives the proposed legislation hoped to accomplish, while yet another qualified the expressed commitment in Goodwin draft's to the rights of free speech and assembly by noting that citizens must exercise them responsibly, with regard to "the constitutional rights of our neighbors."

Following the completion of editorial changes to Goodwin's draft, an unknown aide prepared the president's reading copy of the speech, making two small changes in the process. The first was an insignificant alteration in the phrasing. The second was the minor addition of a brief passage expressing the president's gratitude "for the opportunity to come here tonight to reason with my friends and former colleagues" and noting that he wanted to discuss "briefly the main proposals of this legislation."

Despite the completion of the reading copy, the speechwriting process was not yet at an end, as President Johnson's ad-libbing during his delivery constituted improvisational speechwriting. Mostly, LBJ made minor word substitutions and added short phrases to reduce his reliance on the manuscript, but he also added one piece of information that likely came available only following the completion of the reading copy: "The broad principles of [the voting rights] bill will be in the hands of the Democratic and Republican leaders tomorrow. After they have reviewed it, it will come here formally as a bill." Another addition attempted to forge an identification with President Lincoln, one of Johnson's favorite rhetorical strategies when speaking about issues of racial justice: "It was more than a hundred years ago that Abraham Lincoln . . . signed the Emancipation Proclamation, but emancipation is a proclamation and not a fact." The most common feature of the more significant comments LBJ improvised, however, was their focus on the president. Some of the additions were self-referential in a benign way: He added the introductory phrase "I would like to caution you and remind you" to one of his appeals. However, most of his extemporization seems designed to call attention to his personal efforts, struggles, power, desires, and ambitions: Considered collectively, it imbued the speech with a sense of egotism that in places tarnishes its message. For example, when summarizing civil rights laws already on the books, LBJ apparently could not resist adding that he had "helped to put three of them there." When reflecting on the current civil rights challenge, he intimated that he personally bore "the problems of our country" and emphasized that there "have been many pressures upon your President." He punctuated his passionate call to "root out injustice" with the sentence "Your president makes that request of every American." At the end of a heartfelt passage about his desire to use his authority to effect racial change, he altered the phrasing so that it devolved into an invitation to the listener to become complicit in Johnson's private, ego-driven campaign against injustice. Finally, although Goodwin's draft twice used the narcissistic phrase "I want to be the president who" to introduce Johnson's vision for his achievements, LBJ employed the phrase three additional times during his delivery and expanded his utopian vision to include being the president that helped bring about "love among the people of all races." Johnson's improvisation during his delivery of the address constituted more than a personalization of the speech's language and style to make it his own; rather, he refashioned the text to update its information, alter its appeals, and feature himself.[13]

In the end, the speech Lyndon Johnson delivered on March 15, 1965, was not radically different from its first draft. Though White House aides wrote and edited the speech in haste, the prepared message fitted LBJ's rhetorical style and his apparent rhetorical intentions. Even though the principals involved in the preparation of the address (except Jack Valenti) stop short of calling the speech perfect, none believes the speech should have been fundamentally different, even though most wish it could have been shorter. Nevertheless, the message about voting rights prepared by White House aides and ad-libbed by Johnson would have failed miserably to connect with its listeners had rhetorical timing deviated any further from perfection.

Timing

Because President Johnson did not finalize his plans to deliver a major speech until a full week after the Bloody Sunday attack, the moment for a fitting rhetorical resolution of the voting rights exigency seemed almost to have passed. On the morning of March 15, the *Christian Science Monitor* reported that the White House was "trying rather desperately to keep one jump ahead of national indignation over the civil rights crisis in Selma." LBJ himself claimed that he felt compelled to convince Americans that the administration was "moving as far and as fast as [it] could." Johnson's press conference remarks and written statements had thus far failed to satisfy citizens' and activists' desire that he deliver a strong statement to reestablish some sense of normal politics and normal time. Many believed him to be lagging behind public sentiment and not moving as quickly as he should. To the extent that this belief caused them to lose faith in the president's leadership and the federal government's ability to solve the problem of voter discrimination, the opportune time for speaking seemed to have gone by. And for those who believed President Johnson would already have spoken out if he were genuinely committed to civil rights, the appropriate time for speaking also seemed to have slipped away.[14]

Yet in a sense LBJ could not have spoken sooner even though he worried that the time for crafting a compelling rationale for a national voting rights law out of the immediate crisis might soon pass. That the president's commitment to the issue of voting rights had only recently sharpened kept him from addressing the nation earlier. According to Eric Goldman, President Johnson's personal and political convictions, conception of his office, and impatience merged into an intense desire for action just as he decided when to introduce legislation and whether to speak. In addition, Johnson's political instincts told him to wait for the near completion of the voting rights bill. As a master of political strategy, the president realized that the Selma demonstrations had opened a window of opportunity through which he could push strong legislation, but he hoped the window would stay open long enough for his administration to complete a solid draft of such a measure.[15] Thus, a March 15 presidential address on voting rights seemed well timed when located both on a timeline charting Johnson's commitment and political preparations and on a broader timeline plotting the evolution of federal civil rights policy. However, when considered during a period of heightened emotions precipitated by an immediate crisis, Johnson's speech seemed to come too late. For LBJ to succeed in his voting rights message, then, he needed to use language to reconfigure his listeners' perception of time in a way that made his address seem timely.

Since its delivery, scholars and commentators have regularly judged the "We Shall Overcome" speech as "perfect" in its timing. But this judgment was cultivated, I believe, by President Johnson's achievement in using rhetoric to provide a well-timed, fitting sense of closure to the historical events that led the American public to demand new a voting rights statute. Johnson's speech was fit for the occasion not because of its moment of delivery but rather because it was an effective rhetorical intervention into a complex historical configuration of people, events, and ideas related to voting rights—one that reshaped many of his listeners' perceptions and thus altered that configuration to fit the president's political purposes. Induced to see the urgent situation triggered by the Selma protests from a different temporal perspective, LBJ's listeners were also coached to participate in the resolution of this national urgency by supporting the president's legislative initiatives.

Conclusion

What seems obvious now—that delivering a national address on the issue of voting rights was the right course of action for President Johnson—was not clear to decision makers in March of 1965. LBJ made a firm decision, though, despite the context of uncertainty—and had faith that his choice would turn out to be the right one for both the nation and himself. Indeed, Johnson's address stands as a highly effective rhetorical intervention into a complex exigency. The events in Selma elicited strong reactions from many Americans but were not accompanied by a clear sense of what should be done to restore order and to right a serious wrong. Before his address, some citizens charged that the president had not responded quickly enough to this urgent situation, yet most still looked to him to make sense of it and provide direction. After weeks of overseeing the preparation of a variety of messages on voting rights, Johnson believed that his speechwriters would craft a speech that would do exactly that. His faith was not misplaced, as his voting rights address provided a masterful interpretation that helped achieve a significant political good.

CHAPTER FIVE

"We Shall Overcome"

Much more than an effective compendium of President Johnson's ideas on voting rights fitted to his manner of speaking, the "We Shall Overcome" speech effectively leveraged and transcended the exigencies of the moment to advance a compelling argument for strong, federal voting rights legislation. Along the way, LBJ also reaffirmed the nation's political commitments and the right of every citizen, regardless of race, to enjoy the benefits of democracy in the United States. The president's speech was timely. It was demanding and deliberate. It was personal, principled, and plain spoken. Moreover, it is an exemplary instance of political oratory that deserves close attention.

The Text

We begin with a more intensive study of how the speech directs itself toward time, since all exemplary oratory must possess what the ancient Greeks called *kairos,* or "fitness for the occasion," mastery of the moment. Other rhetorical features of the "We Shall Overcome" address also helped make the principle of equal voting rights meaningful and compelling, but the speech's most significant rhetorical feat lies perhaps in mastering the moment by transforming its hearers' sense of time. The message expands listeners' perceptions of time in the text by forging a connection to the mythic past: The purpose of this expansion is to restructure their perception of time in the world of public affairs to make an immediate solution to the problem of voter discrimination seem prudent. Communication scholar Thomas Farrell observes that, in regard to rhetoric, prudence in the world of public affairs involves enacting practical wisdom (*phronesis*) through the timely choice (*kairos*) of collaborative agents. Much of the rhetorical force of LBJ's voting rights address comes from inviting his listeners to exercise good judgment at a moment he rhetorically constitutes as the right time.[1]

President Johnson begins his message with a sentence that suggests his speech will transcend the immediate urgency: "I speak tonight for the dignity of man and the destiny of democracy." Following a sentence urging unity, he implies that the problems embodied in the Selma situation go beyond time: "At times history and fate meet at a single time in a single place to shape a turning point in man's unending search for freedom. So it was at Lexington and Concord. So it was a century ago at Appomattox. So it was last week in Selma, Alabama."

He invites his audience to look beyond the immediate moment to make sense of the urgency confronting the nation. In short, Johnson rhetorically transforms the confrontation in Selma from an event in ordinary time into one of mythic time. Though he briefly invokes a universal mythos (i.e., "man's unending search for freedom"), he focuses on the part of that quest undertaken in the United States. As such, he suggests that the confrontation in Selma should be seen not as an immediate, isolated struggle but rather as bound up with the great struggles in U.S. history: the fight for independence, the trial of the Union. Furthermore, by naming the sites of this mythic struggle, he binds time and space—an essential rhetorical act for creating and sustaining mythical consciousness. As described by President Johnson, the present represents more than just a moment of opportunity; it is also a moment that allows Americans to see that they stand at a crossroads. Selma is a place where the trajectories of history and destiny have intersected for just a moment and thus demands reckoning.[2]

After this invocation, Johnson describes the recent events in Selma in more ordinary language: "There, long-suffering men and women peacefully protested the denial of their rights as Americans. Many were brutally assaulted. One good man, a man of God, was killed." He then contends that, more importantly than outraging the nation's conscience, the offenses in Selma have stained the nation's character. Americans cannot be proud, he suggests, given the violence committed against protestors. Rather, they should be ashamed, given "the long denial of equal rights of millions of Americans." Johnson implies that the transgressions in Selma will bring about a loss of hope and faith in democracy unless the U.S. government takes decisive action. He transforms Selma from a site that has revealed the evils of Southern racists (whom LBJ strategically avoids naming as agents of violence; instead, protestors "were brutally assaulted" and a minister "was killed") into a fault in the American landscape. Fortunately, Johnson claims, the nation can repair this flaw through immediate legislative action. He claims that "what is happening here tonight"—the beginnings of historical and legal reckoning by the nation's legislative body—will mend democracy and restore the faith of citizens. LBJ again binds time and space, this time emphasizing the here and now. In addition, since Selma is bound up with both the present day and the mythic past, the present becomes more than just a moment of immediate urgency; it is in actuality one of the nation's "moments of great crisis." By asking legislators and citizens to "join me in that cause" (the cause of equal rights) and investing the place and moment of the speech with a mythic presence, the president invites listeners to reconfirm their commitment to democratic principles and bear witness to the vitality of democracy in the United States.

The very beginning of this speech has transformed an acute political problem into something even grander: The effort to solve it becomes a "cause" taken up at a "turning point" and has acquired an almost religious dimension since it involves Americans' "destiny" and "faith." As Johnson continues, this quasi-religious dimension of his claims becomes more pronounced. The current state of affairs, he suggests, is not marked merely as special but rather as sacred. LBJ does not simply state that the protests in Selma have moved the government to act; instead, he claims that the "hymns . . . of oppressed people have summoned [it] into convocation." What he describes in the speech's second sentence as a "cause" to ensure equal rights, he soon describes as part of the nation's "mission."

Johnson's quasi-religious claims and language are rooted in the cultural tradition scholars usually refer to as civil religion—the collection of symbols, beliefs, values, and rituals that give sacred meaning to secular political life; the transcendent sense of reality through which the nation interprets its historical experience. Central to this civil religion are three myths: (1) that the United States has a covenant that makes its citizens a chosen people; (2) that the United States has a special purpose—to be the paragon of liberty and republican governance; and (3) that the nation's founding was not a mere social charter but rather a sacred act (expressed in sacred texts—the Declaration of Independence and the Constitution) that defined the meaning of the United States. Throughout U.S. history, political orators have grounded their reformist appeals in civil religion, recalling Americans to their original task, reminding them of their sins and the wages of sin, and pointing out the path to redemption.[3] In his invocation of the civil religious tradition, LBJ contextualizes the contemporary struggle over voting as part of a transhistorical struggle for the United States to maintain its covenant, to live out its purpose, and to honor its origin. The president coaches his audience to experience current events as part of a transcendent reality.

Johnson begins by giving the issue of equal voting rights mythic significance and then invests this mythos with a religious dimension. He claims that equal voting rights constitute an issue at the "heart of America itself," one bound up with "the values and the purposes and the meaning of our beloved nation." To fail to secure this right, he argues, would constitute more than just a political breakdown; rather, it would mean that Americans had "failed as a people and as a nation." In warning the nation of the consequences of such a failure, the president invokes a passage from the Bible, Luke 9:2, cautioning that it would "lose [its] own soul." He suggests that America's loss would be so deep because guaranteeing liberty and equality are among the fundamental goals of "the first nation in the history of the world to be founded with a purpose." Johnson induces his listeners to want to guarantee equal voting rights in order to honor their status as a chosen people and to live out their sacred purpose.

LBJ's description of that sacred purpose is a bit convoluted, but in essence he suggests it is to uphold a republic model of government committed to liberty and equality. In explicating this purpose, he invokes the mythos of America's origin, quoting from and paraphrasing portions of the Declaration of Independence. By claiming that maxims from the nation's founding—"All men are created equal" and "government by consent of the governed"—still "sound in every American heart," the president makes the mythical past a part of the present while intimating that supporting voting rights legislation is a way to ensure that those maxims are "not just clever words" or expressions of "empty theories." He claims that these principles, established at the founding, were a promise of liberty and equality to all Americans in all times. Failing to keep this promise by discriminating on the basis of race, he argues, would negate the very meaning of the nation and the death of its martyrs: It would be "to deny America" and "to dishonor the dead who gave their lives for American freedom."

Johnson ends the opening section of his address—which, as we have seen, focuses on the meaning of the country and its present crisis—by putting a point on how the past should determine a course of action for the present. Underscoring the significance of the nation's founding, he observes that "our fathers" held that "the right to choose your own leaders" was the fundamental right of our democracy, a government dedicated to the "rights of man." The nation has made steady progress toward its purpose, he suggests: "The history of this country, in large measure, is the history of the expansion of that right [the right to vote] to all of our people." He claims that the present course of action is thus clear: "There is no duty that weighs more heavily on us than the duty we have to ensure that right."

Though President Johnson's civil religious appeals are concentrated at the beginning of the text, they reappear in two key passages. First, near the middle of the address, Johnson claims that the promise of liberty made at the nation's founding was fortified during a second time of trial: "It was more than a hundred years ago that Abraham Lincoln . . . signed the Emancipation Proclamation, but emancipation is a proclamation and not a fact. A century has passed, more than a hundred years, since equality was promised. And yet the Negro is not equal. A century has passed since the day of promise. And the promise is unkept. The time of justice has now come. . . . It is right in the eyes of man and God that it should come."

Johnson invokes the name of a figure widely regarded as an American martyr and uses a sacred text as evidence even though the Emancipation Proclamation did not promise the civil rights he suggests. In this passage LBJ again connects the mythical past to the present by urging citizens to keep the sacred promises made during the nation's time of trial. Moreover, he invests the present moment with a sense of historical gravity that makes immediate action seem natural, right, and overdue. In a second passage weighted with civil religious meaning, the Judeo-Christian character of his appeal is more explicit: "Above the pyramid on the great seal of the United States, it says . . . 'God has favored our undertaking.' God will not favor everything we do. It is rather our duty to divine His will. But I cannot help believing that He truly understands and that He really favors the undertaking that we begin here tonight." Here, in the final words of the address, Johnson reminds Americans of their special purpose and takes on the role of the nation's prophet, suggesting that he has intuited the will of God to be on the side of federal voting rights legislation. He suggests that, by enacting such legislation, the United States can confirm its covenant relationship with the Divinity.

The opening section of President Johnson's speech, as well as the two later passages that also feature civil religious appeals, are crucial to its rhetorical force. In short, LBJ argues that the political crisis raised by the Selma demonstrations is not ephemeral but rather eternal because of its centrality to the American promise and purpose. Though the crisis itself did not possess sacred meaning, Johnson ascribes it and argues that this deeper, transcendent meaning points to the need for an immediate, definitive solution to the problem of voter discrimination. For listeners persuaded by the president's rhetorical strategy of putting this immediate political problem in a mythical, quasi-religious context, supporting voting rights legislation becomes a way to help the nation stay true to its sacred promise and purpose.

Rhetorical theorist Kenneth Burke calls the context in which a speaker locates a subject (and, in effect, defines its meaning) its circumference. In any given rhetorical encounter, a speaker has a great variety of circumferences from which to select when defining a given subject, and the varying scopes lead listeners to different judgments about that subject. The skillful manipulation of circumference is crucial for shaping an audience's interpretations of the people, actions, and motives of any particular situation.[4] President Johnson could have located the struggle for voting rights in a much different circumference—the historical efforts to expand the right to vote, the constitutional provisions for access to the ballot box, or the immediate causes of this crisis (i.e., the intransigence and brutality of government officials in Selma), but emphasizing the history of the expansion of the franchise would have revealed that the trajectory toward guaranteeing equal voting rights was not straight and true. Focusing on the Constitution would have thrust him into a tedious legal argument about voting rights with Southern racists. Focusing on the immediate crisis would have made him vulnerable to charges that he was acting in haste in response to an aberrant situation.

Instead, Johnson chose the circumference of "the American promise," the title he assigned to this speech. His strategy of framing support for federal voting rights legislation as support for the American promise had significant rhetorical advantages. First, it made opposition to voting rights legislation seem un-American. To counter this, opponents would need to argue in effect that voter discrimination is consistent with American values—a general proposition unbelievable to most citizens, including a good number of Southerners. Second, Johnson's rhetorical strategy enabled him to avoid making a philosophical argument on behalf of voting rights. Instead of making his own natural rights argument for fully equal voting rights, he asserts that extending the franchise to all citizens is consistent with the Founders' promise that all citizens will "share in the dignity of man." This assertion is a substitute for argument and endeavors to use listeners' respect for the Founding Fathers and faithfulness to the myth of America to commit them to comprehensive voting rights legislation. As we saw in chapter one, LBJ's assertion is false, as most of the Founders did not view voting as a natural right or see all citizens as fit for voting. Nevertheless, the president's privilege as the nation's interpreter-in-chief gave him rhetorical power with many listeners to explain what the Founders would think about a contemporary political issue. Moreover, an argument rooted in the American mythos promised to be more effective with most of his audience than an abstract, complicated argument about natural rights.

Locating the exigency facing the nation in the context of the American promise was an astute rhetorical move. President Johnson coached listeners to see the urgency as a mythic moment inviting quick, decisive action rather than political wrangling. This scope emphasizes who Americans are, outlines what they should do to resolve the crisis, and makes clear why they should do it. LBJ's invitation is appealing: He calls on Americans to see themselves as a chosen people endeavoring to sustain democratic governance in order to live out their covenant. Johnson and his speechwriters must have hoped that this myth of America would transcend the political quarrelling triggered by the Selma demonstrations and rise above racial and partisan ideologies. In addition, activating this myth gave citizens an opportunity to salve their consciences following a moment marked by shame. The president's speech served a quasi-religious function for some citizens by allowing them to purge their guilt over the violence in Selma and atone for the sins of racial discrimination. Johnson's transformation of a political act—the support of comprehensive federal voting rights legislation—into a transcendent, mythic, quasi-religious act is perhaps this speech's most remarkable rhetorical feat.

The circumference of the American promise is also vital to the speech's timing, its apparent fitness for the occasion. The primary temporal rhetoric of President Johnson's address involves defining the meaning of current events—and thus what constitutes a fitting response to the crisis triggered by the violence in Selma—relative to mythic time and space. The speech thus functions as a ritual for effecting the passage from profane to sacred time. In doing so, LBJ transforms the nature of the urgency. Following Bloody Sunday, violence was the feature of this political crisis with the strongest presence. However, Johnson does not focus on the profane: His speech lacks a vivid evocation or reminder of the brutality against protestors. Instead, he gives sacred American ideals a stronger presence, a compelling immediacy. By taking listeners out of time to a point of mythic, historical reckoning that presents itself "rarely in any time," the president makes political action seem urgent but abates the sense of panic marking the situation. His characterization of the urgency as possessed of aspects that are timeless (i.e., marked by transcendent ideals), timely (e.g., "The time of justice has now come"), and behind time (e.g., "A century has passed. And the promise is unkept") gives the speech a complex timing well suited to the rhetorical situation he faced. As its speaker has his eye on transcendent matters, the address does not seem overdue. As he locates the voting rights crisis on a broad historical timeline, LBJ forestalls criticism that he is moving too fast on civil rights. Indeed, he transforms listeners' sense of time to make immediate action seem prudent not because it aims to resolve an immediate panic or dispute (which fit with the president's desire to avoid sending troops to Selma) but rather because it represents an enactment of America's long-standing, sacred resolve to uphold liberty and equality. Even when he argues the issue of haste more pointedly elsewhere in the address, he does not advance an argument from expediency. About a third of the way through the address, Johnson states, "This time, on this issue, there must be no delay or no hesitation." Yet he counsels against delay because, he suggests, waiting to pass legislation would amount to a "compromise with our purpose." And when he argues that "we ought not and we cannot and we must not wait another eight months before we get a bill," he immediately relates his call for swiftness to America's promise: "We have already waited a hundred years and more, and the time for waiting is gone."

After contextualizing the contemporary political crisis as part of the American promise and refashioning his audience's sense of time, Johnson turns to a discussion of the details of voter discrimination. Employing a problem-cause-solution organizational strategy common to policy address, in this section LBJ explains the methods of voter discrimination, the reasons it happens, and what must be done to stop it.

Johnson describes the political problem succinctly. He states that, although the right to vote is sacred in the United States, "the harsh fact is that in many places in this country men and women are kept from voting simply because they are Negroes." LBJ's language is strategically indirect here, however, as he uses the passive voice rather than naming the agents who keep African Americans from voting. This passive construction and his use of the phrase "in many places" seems designed to avoid indicting the South directly, in an effort to avoid exacerbating regional divisions and irritating Southerners. Still, Johnson does not avoid describing the means of discrimination employed by racist voting officials in the South: Using the descriptions from Horace Busby's speech draft, he outlines how "every device of which human ingenuity is capable has been used" to keep African Americans from voting. He relates how officials kept blacks from attempting to register through deception, telling hopeful applicants that they had missed the registration day, they had arrived too late, or the registrar was not present. He recounts how registrars arbitrarily disqualified blacks for minor, inconsequential omissions or mistakes on their applications, such as abbreviating a word. He mentions that registrars also used onerous, immaterial tests—such as asking applicants to recite the entire Constitution or to explain complex provisions of state law—to disqualify blacks. Then the president rightly emphasizes that these obstacles would not be surmountable if African Americans would just try harder and follow the rules, claiming starkly that "the only way to pass these barriers is to show a white skin." LBJ's description of the methods of voter discrimination is not comprehensive. He does not mention, for example, that black applicants were also turned away for failing to list the county of their birth and for failing to calculate their age to the exact number of days. More importantly, Johnson fails to discuss more extreme, yet common, methods of keeping Southern blacks from voting—intimidation, economic reprisal, and violence. This omission likely reflects his desire to avoid depicting Southern culture as terroristic, vengeful, and violent, as well as his realization that these methods, though made illegal by the White House's legislative proposal, were difficult to prevent and prosecute. Although incomplete, President Johnson's description of the problem still communicates to listeners some sense of the discrimination faced by African Americans.

This communication was important, given the fact that most citizens—and, most likely, many members of Congress—were unaware of the schemes used to keep Southern blacks from voting. The demonstrations in Selma had succeeded in exposing the depths of racism with regard to the vote, a sentiment so deep and strong that many Southerners would engage in violence to maintain supremacy and keep African Americans from petitioning for their constitutional rights. They had not focused attention, however, on the devices used by voter registration boards to keep black applicants from becoming registered voters. In a few of his public statements during the Selma demonstrations, Martin Luther King Jr. claimed that Selma's voter registration test "is so difficult and so ridiculous that even Chief Justice Warren might fail to answer some questions," but the president's expanded and more pointed discussion of registration tests was more effective in highlighting this aspect of voter discrimination.[5] Indeed, Johnson's discussion of the devices of discrimination was important because it emphasized that the nation needed new legislation to stop the machinery of voter discrimination, not mere federal intervention to prevent violence, which would address only the immediate cause of this political crisis.

After outlining the problem that requires resolution through comprehensive federal legislation, Johnson identifies its cause as the shortcomings of "the existing process of law." By highlighting legal deficiencies rather than prejudice as the cause of the problem, he stays focused on his goal of passing new legislation rather than engaging—dangerously—in an argument about the need to exorcise racism from the Southern body politic. LBJ's legislative claims are clear and accurate. He states that existing civil rights laws "cannot overcome systematic and ingenious discrimination," which indeed was true. His emphatic claim that "no law that we now have on the books . . . can ensure the right to vote when local officials are determined to deny it" makes the need for new legislation clear and points out that it was not a lack of enforcement by the executive branch that in effect permitted continued voter discrimination. This claim also undercuts pleas by Southern members of Congress who urged that "existing remedies be given a chance to work" and reinforces his call for immediate action since the passage of time will not remedy a defect in existing civil rights laws.[6]

President Johnson's discussion of a solution is clearly connected to his analysis of the problem and its cause. Most notably, he articulates the purpose and provisions of his proposal, indicating that it will stop the present methods of voter discrimination and prevent further scheming. He also claims that he proposes this solution reluctantly but does so to keep the United States' legal, moral, and political commitments. Moreover, he emphasizes that the government must enact the solution without delay.

Johnson's proposal begins with a clear statement of purpose: The White House voting rights bill is "designed to eliminate illegal barriers to the right to vote." Its main provisions, he claims, will put an end to all restrictions used to keep African Americans from voting in all elections—federal, state, and local; establish a simple, uniform voting formula that cannot be flouted, "however ingenious the effort"; provide for federal voting registrars when state or local officials refuse to register qualified citizens; eliminate "tedious, unnecessary lawsuits" that delay the registration and voting process; and ensure that registered citizens are not kept from voting. He avoids discussing the bill's provisions in detail, which was a smart rhetorical choice, especially since Justice Department officials were still making minor revisions. However, sketching the bill's provisions also made it seem that the White House was providing policy leadership rather than usurping Congress's legislative role: He even invites legislators to suggest ways "to strengthen this law and to make it effective." In addition, a sketch

avoided prompting complaints about specific provisions, especially
its trigger formula, which some civil rights organizations believed was
too restrictive and which some Southerners believed was arbitrary and
designed to penalize the South.

Before making his plea for urgent passage of the voting rights bill,
Johnson suggests that he does not want federal officials to intervene in
state and local elections. "But," he states, "experience has plainly shown
that this is the only path to carry out the command of the Constitution."
He then asserts that, even upon the enactment of comprehensive voting rights legislation, those who oppose federal intervention still have
the power to avoid it. He says, "Open your polling places to all your
people. Allow men and women to register and vote whatever the color
of their skin. Extend the rights of citizenship to every citizen of this
land." This statement represents a sharp rhetorical strategy. Using a line
of argument that emerged during debates about slavery and depicting
themselves as defenders of states' rights, some Southern opponents of
federal voting rights legislation emphasized that they objected to the
measure because it disrupted the normal federal-state relationship.
The president subtly and skillfully undercuts this argument: If voter
discrimination is halted, he declares, the federal government will not
intervene. He suggests that local control over elections will be forfeited
only by illegal, unconstitutional actions undertaken by those who pro-
fess a desire to maintain local control. Two days earlier Johnson had
communicated a similar message to Alabama governor George Wallace
during their meeting at the White House, fixing the responsibility for
outside intervention and "outside agitation" on Southern elected officials and civil servants.[7]

In addition to indicating that states' rights advocates themselves are
responsible for federal intervention, President Johnson suggests that
the doctrine of states' rights itself is wrongheaded and irrelevant when
it comes to solving the problem of voter discrimination: "There is no
constitutional issue here. The command of the Constitution is plain.
. . . There is no issue of states' rights or national rights. There is only
the struggle for human rights." LBJ assumes the political high ground
here rather than arguing his case, as he does when stating that "There

is no moral issue. It is wrong . . . to deny any of your fellow Americans the right to vote."

As we saw in chapter one, the command of the Constitution is not as explicit as he makes it seem. Though the Fifteenth Amendment prevents states from depriving citizens of the vote on the basis of race, it does not actively confer the right to vote, nor does it bar voter restrictions that are not racially discriminatory prima facie. In fact, the members of Congress who adopted the Fifteenth Amendment believed an issue of states' rights was at stake when regulating voting and that it was acceptable to keep some citizens from voting (LBJ, like most political leaders, believed some restrictions on voting to be appropriate). Johnson's statements, then, are flawed because, by containing unconditional claims, they are absolute. His rhetorical strategy seems to be to make it plain that those who engage in race-based voter discrimination are clearly in the wrong. In part, the president was likely trying to demoralize Southern opponents of voting rights legislation by making it seem that a righteous, dedicated force is aligned against them.[8] Such a strategy could also win and energize supporters by making people feel they are on the right side, the side of common sense, the side destined to win. Moreover, strong, absolute assertion rather than nuanced argument conveys the sense that legislation to guarantee equal access to the ballot box will come. LBJ's rhetoric makes the issues involved in solving the problem of voter discrimination seem simple and uncontestable. In contrast, Horace Busby's speech draft contains a focused, more complex argument for federal voting rights legislation based on the Fifteenth Amendment, the history of Congressional intent with regard to eliminating voter discrimination based on race, and the judiciary's interpretation of Constitutional provisions on voting. Busby's arguments are compelling, but Johnson and his advisers probably believed they were ill suited for the president's public speech because they would bog listeners down with constitutional and legislative details rather than providing them with the sense that the issue of voting rights is a simple matter of principle. As such, Busby's arguments appear in the president's written message to Congress but not in his address.

As his discussion of the solution to the voter discrimination problem comes to a close, President Johnson emphasizes the importance
of immediate action. He states plainly that there must be no delay and
that "the time for waiting is gone." He appeals to Americans' sense of
mission, claiming that there must be "no hesitation or no compromise
with our purpose." Johnson also addresses members of Congress directly and asks them to join him in working as long as it takes to pass
the voting rights bill, "to protect the right of every American to vote
in every election." Surprisingly, he does not mention the practical
consequences of delay: that waiting to pass the bill will keep African
Americans from voting in state and local elections. Perhaps he worried that such an appeal would seem too pedestrian coming after such
idealistic rhetoric or too political (i.e., that he was interested in securing
benefits for his party from minority voting). Instead, Johnson ends his
plea for urgency by claiming that it will salve "the outraged conscience
of a nation," abate "the grave concern of many nations," and avoid "the
harsh judgment of history."

After outlining a problem, its cause, and its solution, speakers who
address policy issues often discuss the good that will come from enacting their proposals. Johnson's voting rights address, however, lacks this
rhetorical feature. The absence of a positive vision of an equal opportunity society made possible by equitable voting rights is conspicuous
when one compares his address to the oratory of voting rights activists
and considers his personal convictions. One of the central features of
civil rights oratory was that gaining access to the ballot would lead to
a better, more equal, and more just nation because elected officials
would be beholden to all of their constituents, including African
Americans.

In 1958 King delivered one of the most eloquent speeches containing
these appeals, claiming that blacks will help put an end to lynching, in-
tegrate schools, make the legislature and judiciary more just and moral
political bodies, and restore social order if the federal government will
"give us the ballot." He made similar claims during the Selma protests.
For example, during a February mass meeting at Brown Chapel he declared, "If Negroes could vote, there would be no [Sheriff] Jim Clarks.

There would be no oppressive poverty directed against Negroes. Our children would not be crippled by segregated schools. And the whole community might live together in harmony."[9] President Johnson shared these convictions; he believed that, once African Americans gained the right to vote, "there will be no more of this segregation around here" and that the key to black political and economic equality "has to do with the vote."[10] Yet his address focuses on the gap between the American promise and current political realities and does not suggest that equal access to the ballot will help bring an end to all discrimination, thus creating a more equal and just society. LBJ identifies the problem and suggests the reasons it must be solved, but he does not discuss the political outcomes of enacting his legislative proposal.

Discussing the outcomes of federal voting rights legislation would have given Johnson's speech a more practical dimension by showing that fidelity to the principle of equal voting rights would have real benefits for those previously disenfranchised and help make real many of the other promises of democracy. Instead, his appeals were more idealistic in focusing on the American promise regarding equal voting rights. Yet, in another sense, LBJ's speech was more realistic. Though equal access to the ballot box would bring meaningful political change, it was not a panacea that would create a political utopia, which was the feeling communicated by some voting rights activists and, in private, by the president himself. Perhaps Johnson's speechwriters and editors were more realistic about the power of the vote and thus tempered the idealism of his speech. Although a reference to the benefits of federal legislation would have resonated with black listeners and might have helped secure the support of others, it would have raised expectations beyond what legislation could have achieved, especially in the short run. In addition, such an appeal would have alienated many Southerners: Any suggestion of using the ballot as a tool for dismantling Jim Crow would have been very threatening to Southern segregationists, even those who would not have argued against LBJ's mythic and constitutional claims about the right to vote. Perhaps realizing this, too, Johnson and his aides emphasized the promise and the principle of equal voting rights instead of expressing the president's and the activists' conviction that securing them would effect a radical change in the political culture of the United States.

Though President Johnson's speech is not marked by unrestrained idealism regarding the power of the vote, the address steadily becomes very idealistic with regard to social justice more broadly. After framing the struggle over the right to vote as an endeavor to realize the American promise and outlining the problem of voter discrimination, its cause, and its solution, LBJ becomes more expansive. Indeed, only one brief passage in the remainder of the entire speech deals specifically with the issue of equal voting rights: "Because all Americans just must have the right to vote. And we are going to give them that right." Moving beyond the issue of equal opportunity at the ballot box, the president advocates full civil rights, connects this advocacy to his vision of a Great Society, and eventually suggests that it will take more than just civil rights or equality of opportunity for the United States to realize its potential. Along the way, he also argues that racial discrimination is not strictly a regional problem, commends African American protestors, and discusses the relationship between social protest and law and order. The second half of the address is not organized as clearly as the first half but includes some of the speech's most memorable rhetoric, including the president's statement, "We shall overcome."

Johnson moves beyond the immediate issue of voting rights by locating the struggle for the franchise in a broader context of civil rights advocacy and social progress: "But even if we pass this bill, the battle will not be over. What happened in Selma is part of a far larger movement which reaches into every section and state of America. It is the effort of American Negroes to secure for themselves the full blessings of American life." The president here reminds his listeners that Negroes are Americans, thus making it seem self-evident that they deserve the privileges of citizenship. He also defines the meaning of civil rights protest by naming what it is blacks are striving to achieve. Johnson suggests that African Americans are not fighting to destroy the Southern way of life and are not Communist rabble-rousers; nor are they fighting for a political abstraction. Instead, they are struggling for what every American wants—to enjoy the fruits of American society.

So far, LBJ suggests, blacks have undertaken this great effort themselves. However—addressing members of Congress and his white listeners directly—he claims that all Americans must join in the movement and surmount the problem of racial discrimination: "Their cause must be our cause, too. Because it is not just Negroes, but really it's all of us who must overcome the crippling legacy of bigotry and injustice." Then, in the most remarkable line of the address, Johnson adopts the rallying cry of the civil rights movement to express his conviction that the United States will move beyond its racist past and present: "And we shall overcome."

LBJ's speech does not argue that the ballot will be an instrument for African Americans to destroy Jim Crow; instead, the president calls for a collective effort, spurred along by his leadership, to bring about freedom, equality, and justice. He calls for a reformation of "the attitudes and structures of our society." Moreover, he argues that the American promise demands such a reform and that the need for it is immediate: "The time of justice has now come." Rather than focusing on the benefits to African Americans of a more just society, Johnson claims that it "will brighten the lives of every American." He states that many poor whites are also victims of discrimination and that they suffer from a lack of education and the effects of poverty in part because of the energy wasted "to maintain the barriers of hatred and terror."

LBJ then connects his call for freedom and equality to his broader domestic agenda. Beginning in 1964, the president's speeches began emphasizing that the United States can provide "abundance and liberty for all." He demanded "an end to poverty and racial injustice," claimed that every child should have the opportunity "to enrich his mind and to enlarge his talents," emphasized the need "to give our fellow citizens a fair chance to develop their own capacities," and called for better "education and training" and "medical care" for all citizens. He revisits these themes in the voting rights address: "This great, rich, restless country can offer opportunity and education and hope to all: black and white, North and South, sharecropper and city dweller. These are the enemies: poverty, ignorance, disease. They are the enemies—and not our fellow man, not our neighbor. And these enemies, too—poverty, disease, and ignorance—we shall overcome." Johnson's speech relates the issue of civil rights to broader issues of social justice without subordinating the problem of racial discrimination to other critical problems, which had been a troublesome tendency of many of President Kennedy's speeches on civil rights.[11]

In his call for racial justice as one part of a more equal society, the president avoids isolating the South as an object of criticism. Yet his condemnation of racism in stark language—calling segregationist conventions "barriers of hatred and terror"—must have surprised and outraged many Southern listeners. Further, his assertion that those who "hold on to the past" do so at the expense of their future, is clearly addressed to segregationists in the South, members of Congress and citizens alike. Johnson likely hoped that his personal identification with the South (e.g., his statement that his "roots go deeply into Southern soil") would soften the blow of his rhetoric. Moreover, he attempts to curtail perceptions that he is singling out the South and that the issue of civil rights is a solely Southern problem by identifying inequality as a problem that transcends geography: "Now let none of us in any section look with prideful righteousness on the troubles in another section. . . . There is really no part of America where the promise of equality has been kept." He observes that across the country "Americans are struggling for freedom" and urges Americans everywhere to look within their own hearts and communities and work "to root out injustice wherever it exists." Johnson also attempts to forge a positive identification between the South and the rest of the country by describing how men from all regions have fought together to defend freedom and are fighting together now "without regard to religion or color or region in Vietnam." He then calls on all citizens "from everywhere in this country" to "rally now together in this cause to vindicate the freedom of all Americans."

President Johnson's appeal for a broader campaign of social justice is one of the most inspiring passages of the voting rights address. After having emphasized the centrality of the franchise to democracy in the United States earlier in the address, he calls for more sweeping social change that goes beyond the enactment of American principles, pushing to make the American Dream a reality for all of the nation's people. LBJ expresses confidence that, with the help of all Americans, the nation will overcome its problems and realize a gracious, open future. Though he is less eloquent, he articulates a vision similar to that expressed by Martin Luther King Jr. in his renowned "I Have a Dream" speech at the 1963 March on Washington. Like King, the president envisions the nation living out its promise of equality, securing freedom and justice, and working together for the common good. In addition, LBJ visualizes a society where everyone receives "the full blessings of American life," including education, economic benefit, and good health. In urging his listeners to advance the American ideals of freedom and equality for the benefit of all of the country's citizens, Johnson makes the cause of justice the nation's cause—not just that of civil rights activists. In the process of stirring Americans up about the nation's possibilities and enlisting their support, he makes it fundamentally un-American to oppose the cause of racial justice, including equal voting rights. The president invites his audience to validate its commitment to the American Dream and to participate in the heady project of making the nation all that it can be, which begins with its support of federal legislation to guarantee justice at the ballot box.

President Johnson's effort to assuage regional accusations and re-sentment while advocating justice, however, is not a strong point of the speech. He attempts to forge a personal identification with the South, but it comes across as a futile attempt to head off a backlash from staunch segregationists in Dixieland. He suggests that white Southerners are harmed by segregation, but he fails to identify his aims with those of moderate political and economic leaders in the South who also urged segregationists to move forward on civil rights for their own good. This failure is surprising since he had made exactly this identification with moderate Southerners in a speech in New Orleans on October 9, 1964. Johnson also claims that the issue of civil rights is not a regional prob-lem, but his rhetoric fails to make the point starkly or communicate a sense of urgency. In contrast, in his June 11, 1963, address on civil rights, President Kennedy made the same point more forcefully: "I hope that every American, regardless of where he lives, will stop and examine his

conscience. . . . This is not a sectional issue. Difficulties over segregation and discrimination exist in every city, in every State of the Union,
producing in many cities a rising tide of discontent that threatens the
public safety. . . . It is not enough to pin the blame on others, to say this
is a problem of one section of the country or another, or deplore the
fact that we face. . . . My fellow Americans, this is a problem which faces
us all—in every city of the North as well as the South."

Kennedy's claims had been especially prescient in 1963, but few
heeded his call to focus attention on the problems in urban areas of the
North. Moreover, by 1965, even the Johnson administration still "looked
at the civil rights problem as basically a Southern problem" despite the
fact that "the civil rights problems of the urban ghettos exceeded any
that we were dealing with in the South," according to Deputy Attorney
General Ramsey Clark.[12] The almost token quality of LBJ's statement
that civil rights problems transcend geography perhaps reflects his
preoccupation with Southern civil rights issues and his desire to ap-
pease Southern citizens. It is difficult to say whether more forcefully
calling attention to civil rights problems in other regions would have
made Southerners feel less besieged and whether this effect would have
helped diminish Southern opposition to civil rights legislation in any
case. Nevertheless, by using tepid rhetoric, Johnson clearly missed an
opportunity to make the issue of urban civil rights problems a subject
of national concern before it approached its boiling point just months
later. Finally, punctuating his efforts to counter regional perspectives
and resentment on civil rights with a lifeless claim about all Americans
fighting for freedom around the world has no persuasive potential: It
functions only to make this section of his speech feel even more per-
functory.

Following Johnson's more expansive claims while advocating racial
and social justice—in which he implicitly validates the civil rights movement by adopting one of its rallying calls ("We shall overcome")—the
president commends and supports civil rights activists explicitly. He
also relates civil rights demonstrations to a moderate philosophy of
social protest. Moreover, he charts the landscape on which he believes
democratic social change should take place, plotting out a middle path

between obstructionist dissent and suppressed freedom of speech, between reckless provocation and violent retaliation.

To twenty-first-century listeners and readers, Johnson's description of civil rights activists as heroic, courageous, and brave may seem unremarkable; his claims that protestors had "awakened the conscience of this Nation" may seem commonsensical. To many at the time, however, LBJ's claims were astonishing. He went further than identifying himself and the nation with the movement's aims (which former presidents Truman and Kennedy had also done) to identify "the American Negro" as one of the nation's moral and political redeemers. Guided by their "faith in American democracy," Johnson suggests, black activists had exposed the nation's transgressions and recalled it to its task by urging citizens and elected officials "to make good the promise of America."

Lauding, validating, and perhaps, according to some critics, even encouraging black protest was not a rhetorical feature that promised to connect with many in his audience who were not African American and/or supportive of the civil rights movement. More than any other aspect of the address, Johnson's statements in this vein promised to offend white Southerners. Segregationists had even more animosity toward civil rights activists—labeling them outside agitators, communist inspired, and morally depraved—than their cause. Even Southerners who supported equal voting rights in some measure generally disliked demonstrators and their methods. Moreover, though national opinion polls at the time showed general public support for equal voting rights, they also revealed the public's ambivalence about the civil rights movement. Most notably, polls showed substantial public opposition to direct protest and suggested that "the goals of the civil rights movement enjoy[ed] considerably more social legitimacy than [did] many of the actions . . . utilized by protest groups." The remarks by federal lawmakers recorded in the *Congressional Record* suggest that Congress was also ambivalent toward activists.[13]

Since this rhetorical feature seemed certain to raise the ire of some listeners (e.g., white Southerners), the White House must have believed the president could effect some change in the general public and among members of Congress that would help him achieve his political goals. Johnson and his aides might have hoped that communicating a positive image of the civil rights movement would help sustain public and congressional support for legislation in the long run: Perhaps he reasoned that a positive attitude toward the movement would mean stronger support for the White House's proposal. By emphasizing the motives behind their "actions and protests" and connecting them to the American promise, the president's depiction had some potential to reshape attitudes toward African American activists.

In addition, LBJ likely lauded black activism to cement a relationship with African American leaders that would serve his own political objectives. The Selma demonstrations achieved what the president had urged King to do—use nonviolent action to expose the most outrageous instances of voter discrimination, thus making it possible for the White House to usher new voting rights legislation through Congress. Perhaps Johnson reasoned that presidential validation of black activism and the ensuing benefits of political legitimacy would move civil rights leaders to cooperate further with the president and to press forward with demonstrations that, in his words, aimed only to "call attention," "provoke change," and "stir reform." Moreover, he may have hoped to elicit a favorable emotional response that would head off criticism by civil rights leaders likely to be critical of specific provisions of the White House's legislative proposal.

Perhaps presidential affirmation of the civil rights movement also reflected in some measure the respect LBJ had for activists and certainly sprang from speechwriter Dick Goodwin's personal esteem for those committed to the movement. However, President Johnson's comments that follow suggest still another strategic motive: Having praised moderate protests, he promotes a path of social progress characterized by both "moral right" and "law and order." By claiming that the battle for equality "should be fought . . . in the courts, and in the Congress, and in the hearts of men," the president subtly suggests that demonstrations have a limited, expedient utility. Still, he commits himself to defending "the right to free speech and the right of free assembly" but warns that it must be exercised responsibly: He states that protestors must not infringe on "the constitutional rights of our neighbors." The president also commits himself to supporting local communities' right to enjoy peace, order, and unity. However, he states that the nation will not accept "order imposed by fear" or the suppression of civil rights and the right to protest. By balancing the rights and interests of both sides involved in civil rights controversies, Johnson comes across as a reasonable voice for moderation rather than an unqualified supporter of activists or a chief executive too focused on maintaining order. Indeed, his appeal for unity is sensible and sounds genuine. He emphasizes that everyone in the communities experiencing unrest, including Selma, "must still live and work together" and thus "must try to heal the wounds and to build a new community." Johnson's effort to chart a middle path suggests he appreciated the magnitude of the unstable political exigency he faced. To avoid degenerating from instability into chaos would likely require the kind of balance he advocated.

Following his commentaries on the civil rights movement and the course of social change, President Johnson situates his legislative aims within his expansive vision of a "Great Society." In a passage marked by idealism and realism, he states that the voting rights bill is the start of a civil rights program that aims to "open the city of hope to people of all races." He emphasizes the importance of guaranteeing "the privileges of citizenship regardless of race" but argues that merely securing these rights is not enough. Because of poverty, inadequate education, poor medical care, and inferior housing, Johnson suggests, not all Americans have the capability to exercise their privileges or "contribute to the nation." He claims that "to exercise these privileges takes much more than just legal right," and thus he plans "to give all our people, black and white, the help that they need" to walk though "the gates of opportunity" opened by civil rights legislation. These claims reinforce one of the central themes of Johnson's rhetoric promoting a "Great Society"—that opportunities in the abstract are not meaningful; rather, genuine opportunity requires measures to help citizens benefit from the blessings of the American society. His claims about equal opportunity in this address also foreshadow his redefinition of that concept in a speech at Howard University less than three months later. In that speech he repeats a theme from the voting rights address yet extends his point about equality of opportunity: "[I]t is not enough just to open the gates of opportunity. All our citizens must have the ability to walk through those gates. . . . We seek not just freedom but opportunity. We seek not just legal equity but human ability, not just equality as a right and a theory but equality as a fact and equality as a result."

LBJ declares that his administration aims "to help the American Negro fulfill the rights which, after the long time of injustice, he is finally about to secure. To move beyond opportunity to achievement." Whereas most Americans took the term "equal opportunity" to mean an equal chance to compete for success, Johnson suggested that equal outcomes were the sign of genuine equality of opportunity. His claims about equality in the voting rights address are less challenging to Americans' beliefs than those in his speech at Howard University: He argues for the need to help all citizens exercise their privileges rather than for the need to ensure such benefits. Yet Johnson pushes the concept of equality beyond that articulated by previous presidents, including his immediate predecessor, whose civil rights rhetoric emphasized that "not every child has an equal talent or an equal ability or an equal motivation, but they should have an equal right to develop their talent and their ability and their motivation, to make something of themselves."[14] In contrast, LBJ suggests that the level of one's talent, ability, and motivation is in part the result of socioeconomic privilege or disadvantage; thus he wants to help the disadvantaged develop their aptitudes in order to benefit from the equal opportunities afforded by civil rights legislation.

President Johnson's advocacy of his vision of a Great Society seems designed to secure support for his domestic agenda and to help him assume a stronger leadership role in civil rights. Like his discussion of voting rights, the president's claims about the need for equal opportunity are rooted in the American Dream. His assertion that he wants to give citizens the help they need to realize the benefits of American society is heady and seems poised to elicit positive sentiments for his vision for domestic policy: He speaks about the potential pitfalls of life in the United States yet is optimistic that they can be overcome; he appeals to shared values rather than confronting them (i.e., he does not promise to guarantee equal success) to commit citizens to the cause of genuine opportunity. In addition to connecting with many listeners' faith in the American Dream, LBJ's claims about opportunity were crafted to connect with an emerging belief among civil rights activists that the movement needed to become concerned "not merely with removing the barriers to full opportunity but with achieving the fact of equality."[15] By articulating this emerging concern before the movement had effectively expressed it to the public, Johnson may have hoped to lead the civil rights movement rather than responding to its initiatives and the political crises they might trigger.

After including the audience in his appeal to grant all citizens the chance to enjoy the benefits of American life ("So *we* want to open the gates to opportunity. But *we* are also going to give all our people ... the help they need to walk through those gates" [emphasis added]), LBJ turns his focus inward on himself. Rather than fleshing out his vision of a nation in which lawmakers reach across party lines and citizens bridge the divisions of race and class to build a better society, Johnson articulates a vision of a Great Society made real by presidential feats. He begins humbly enough by describing the disadvantage and discrimination endured by the Mexican American students he taught during his first job in Cotulla, Texas. A listener might have imagined LBJ using this anecdote to illustrate his earlier point that poverty keeps people from enjoying the privileges of citizenship, but instead the president uses it to emphasize his own desire and efforts to help the downtrodden. Johnson suggests that as a teacher he did what little he could to help his students "face the hardships that lay ahead" and is now eager to seize the opportunity "to help the sons and daughters of those students and to help people like them all over this country." He makes a short statement urging the audience to join him in accepting the opportunity to help the disadvantaged, but it is preceded and followed by statements that call attention to his own exercise of power. In a passage that describes his presidential ambitions, he abandons the restraint that characterizes much of the address. Johnson tends toward self-absorption, and his aspirations sound unrealistic: "I want to be the president who educated young children to the wonders of their world. I want to be the president who helped to feed the hungry and to prepare them to be taxpayers instead of taxeaters. I want to be the president who helped the poor find their own way and who protected the right of every citizen to vote in every election. I want to be the president who helped to end hatred among his fellow men and who promoted love among the people of all races and all regions and all parties. I want to be the president who helped to end war among the brothers of this earth."

Although Dick Goodwin wrote the foundation for this passage, it still reveals aspects of the president's psychology. It is especially reve-latory of Johnson's preoccupation with his place in history and with how he would be remembered. LBJ often worried that the conflict in Vietnam would overshadow his accomplishments. Given the U.S. mili-tary escalation in Vietnam following the attack at Pleiku in February of 1965, perhaps LBJ hoped this speech would redirect attention—both immediate and historical—on his vision, especially of domestic af-fairs. The language of this section seems designed to induce a peculiar state of reflection on accomplishments yet to come: He uses the past tense ("helped") to make his ambitions sound like achievements and describes himself as "the president" rather than using the first-person pronoun ("I want to help ..."). He could have deployed his preoccupa-tion with history rhetorically as he did in his White House meeting with George Wallace, during which he suggested that, since progress on civil rights was certain, the governor had the power to determine how he would be remembered by history: as a leader who looked to the future or as a hater mired in the past. Instead of expressing his own desires (which had little, if any, persuasive potential), President Johnson might have again described the present as a moment of historical reckoning and asked his audience, "How do we want to be remembered by his-tory—as a people who recommitted the United States to its promise and helped build a better nation or as people who shirked their duty and let an opportunity for greatness pass by?"

After this passage focusing on his ambitions, LBJ addresses the legislators directly in the conclusion and returns to his central theme. First, he invites senators and congressmen "to share this [task] with me and to share it with the people that we both work for" and states that he wants "this to be the Congress" that helps the nation achieve its potential. Still, he positions himself as the nation's legislative leader, undermining his initial rhetorical plan to avoid the impression that he was usurping the Congress's power. Whereas the prepared copy of the speech asks legislators to share their task with him, Johnson's ad-libbing during the delivery turns this request on its head. He then recalls the Congress to its central task of serving the needs of its constituents: He declares that, although citizens bear their burdens alone and rely on themselves along life's way, they also "look to each of us" for help. In his final words, the president revisits his central theme of the American promise: He identifies the effort to ensure equal voting rights and to secure civil rights, guarantee equal opportunity, and advance the cause of human fellowship as one favored by the Divine. He invokes the mythos of God's special covenant with the United States and intuits for his listeners that God "really favors the undertaking that we begin here tonight."

Having in the second half of his address brought the immediate case for voting rights outward, into an expanded time and place where securing civil rights was but a first step toward a "Great Society," President Johnson's conclusion reconnects with the rhetorical strategies of the speech's first half. He once again focuses America's ideals and history inward to bring them to bear on the immediate, fundamental task of guaranteeing equal access to the ballot box for all of the nation's citizens. Linking transcendent values with particular action, he invites his listeners to participate in a political act of fulfillment and redemption.

Conclusion

By writing the present into the story of the American promise, LBJ makes the principle of equal voting rights salient and meaningful. His mythic appeals identify the right to vote as central to the meaning of the nation. Thus, the struggle to guarantee equal access to the ballot box becomes a crusade to honor the country's covenant and live up to its purpose, not merely an effort to redress the political wrong committed against African Americans in Selma. Johnson's assertion that the phrase "government by consent of the governed" is not just a catchy slogan or an empty theory is borne out as his rhetoric makes the principle of equal voting rights real for his listeners. Moreover, by refashioning their sense of time, he makes his rhetorical action seem timely and legislative action appear pressing. These rhetorical feats were achieved in part by grounding his appeals in the tradition of American civil religion, which provided him with a public vocabulary of shared interests, motives, and aspirations. To forge a moral consensus requires a vocabulary of moral consensus. The vocabulary of American civil religion that assigns negative meanings to actions that threaten the nation's covenant, undermine its purpose to be the paragon of liberty and republican governance, or violate the principles of its sacred texts is wrong. LBJ uses this vocabulary to argue that voter discrimination is unethical and must be stopped because it undercuts the American promise; as such, his rhetoric transcends differences of sentiment related to racial bias.

In addition to interpreting current events using the frame of the American promise, President Johnson interprets them by defining the problem facing the nation, its cause, and its solution. His speech is crafted to avoid alienating Southern listeners and to address the audience's concerns about the need for the president's proposed legislation. Though many Americans demanded presidential action following the Selma crisis, legislative action was not the only proposal that might have satisfied their demands: LBJ could have made a compelling address that presented a plan for federal protection of civil rights workers, more vigorous prosecution of voting rights cases (recently made easier by Supreme Court rulings), and greater compliance with existing civil rights laws. However, because he believed such a measure would be more effective, would stand as a stronger symbol of his commitment to equal rights, and would help ensure his place in history, he wanted to secure passage of voting rights legislation. Thus, in describing the means of voter discrimination, he suggests that federal protection will not solve the core problem that triggered a national exigency. He argues that previous civil rights laws have significant shortcomings in regard to the franchise; more time for compliance and enforcement, he suggests, will not solve the problem of voter discrimination. Furthermore, throughout the problem-cause-solution section of the speech he attempts to head off Southern antagonism by focusing on the acts of voter discrimination rather than on the agents who commit them and by suggesting that Southern states can avoid federal intervention in elections by stopping unconstitutional electoral practices.

Johnson's problem-cause-solution arguments represent constructive rhetorical leadership. He assumes a teaching role for the public by providing an accurate reading of conditions in the South and clearly describing his plan of action. Even though his depiction of voter discrimination is abridged and strategic, he avoids simplifying the issue and clouding the public's judgment. If his claim about the absence of a constitutional or states' rights issue is too absolute, it was only because he believed the legislation carefully prepared by the Justice Department would sidestep those issues. Though he does not provide a detailed constitutional analysis of the right to vote, his strong assertion that American ideals are on the side of equal voting rights is a sincere, accurate interpretation of constitutional doctrine and national principles. LBJ's request for immediately enacting a solution to the problem of voter discrimination is admirable, as he does not advocate haste for the purpose of resolving the immediate crisis but rather for the redress of a long-running deficiency of principle. Moreover, the president's rhetorical leadership demonstrates foresight, for as he describes the solution to the problem of voter discrimination, he employs not only rhetorical strategies designed to help pass the voting right bill but also an approach crafted to encourage compliance following the law's enactment.

President Johnson's address also provides a skilled interpretation by situating the immediate exigency within a broader political struggle. He asserts that the campaign to secure equal voting rights is part of a larger effort to secure civil rights across the board. Moreover, his proposal to guarantee equal voting rights is a first step in a program to help achieve social justice and realize its potential in a Great Society. LBJ's more expansive rhetoric is still strategic in its attempt to obtain support for his legislative proposal. He relates the effort to acquire equal rights to the American Dream by describing its goal as realizing "the full blessings of American life," which in effect characterizes opposition to this legislation as un-American. He claims that eliminating discrimination and advancing social justice will benefit all Americans—not just blacks—and suggests that citizens should not look down on the South since civil rights problems exist everywhere. He depicts civil rights activists in a positive way that reinforces the rightness of their cause, to which he invites all citizens to commit themselves. And in describing his plan for a Great Society, the president positions himself as a strong yet moderate leader on civil rights.

In relating the struggle for voting rights to a plan for a more equal and more just nation, Johnson communicates an idealistic, inspiring vision. He imparts a compelling emotional life to the political and cultural tradition that undergirded the appeals in the first half of the address. LBJ urges the citizenry to become better than it is and expresses optimism about what the United States can be. His vision is challenging yet grounded in shared values. And the president's rhetoric is prudent, at least for most of the address. His optimistic proposal to bring the benefits of the United States to more of its citizens is tempered by a sense of what can be achieved. However, Johnson then lists his presidential ambitions, beginning with goals that are attainable (e.g., helping "to feed the hungry") but ending with claims wholly lacking in prudence (e.g., "I want to be the president who helped to end hatred among his fellow men and . . . who helped to end war among the brothers of this earth"). Although President Johnson enacts one of his worst rhetorical habits by focusing attention on himself and suggesting unrealistic achievements, the overall tone of the address is still inspiring, demanding, and judicious.

At the close of the address, LBJ assumes a strong leadership role. He asks members of Congress to join him in serving the citizenry and in making the American promise a reality. Scholars of the rhetorical presidency have rightly noted that chief executives should be cautious about publicly urging the passage of specific legislation in order to avoid usurping Congress's role and limiting deliberation.[16] However, this case benefited from Johnson's very public rhetorical leadership. None of the numerous voting rights bills introduced by legislators in the weeks prior to his address had gained momentum in the Congress. LBJ's speech jump-started the legislative process. Congress would have been unable to fully resolve the national exigency since many citizens looked to the president to express the government's commitment to civil rights and to show that the government would soon enact a solution. Johnson's speech helped soothe legitimate public concern. Congress had deliberated the issue of equal voting rights for many years (including a recent debate preceding the passage of the Civil Right Act of 1964) and was unlikely to achieve a new level of consensus. LBJ's speech set a high standard for voting rights legislation and put pressure on recalcitrant members of Congress who were unwilling to guarantee the command of the Fifteenth Amendment. Yet the president did not railroad the Congress, as he included many legislators in the process of drafting the voting rights bill and in his speech invited proposals to strengthen the measure.

Johnson's address is a significant instance of rhetorical leadership. Without it, the Voting Rights Act would likely have been weakened and delayed. His message helped solidify the supporters of comprehensive voting rights legislation, was positioned to gain new supporters by changing what it meant to back such legislation, and helped demoralize the opponents of equal rights. In the next chapter I examine the way in which some of the president's listeners responded to his speech in order to understand its rhetorical action and to gauge, in a limited sense, the extent to which his rhetoric induced audience members to understand the crisis confronting the nation differently and motivated them to act differently.

CHAPTER SIX

Praise and Rebuke

Lyndon Johnson's voting rights address received widespread attention. A national audience of seventy million watched the speech on
television. Scores of national and local newspapers and magazines
reprinted either full-text or abridged versions of the message. Upon the
demand of their readers, some African American newspapers, including the *Norfolk Journal and Guide* and the *Philadelphia Afro-American*,
reprinted the text of the president's address the following week. One
leading black newspaper, the *Chicago Defender*, even prepared an
offprint for free distribution to its readers. The speech also reached a
sizeable international audience: A few newspapers, including the *Times*
(London) and *Tanjug* (Belgrade), printed complete transcripts; several
European, African, Asian, and Latin American publications reprinted
excerpts of the address; and the Voice of America broadcast portions
of the speech as part of its global programming.

Having seen, heard, or read Johnson's speech, thousands of Americans—including everyday citizens, opinion leaders, and political fig-
ures—felt strongly enough about the message to write to the president
and express their reactions to his words. The archives at the Lyndon B.
Johnson Library contain more than 13,400 pieces of opinion mail and
telegrams responding specifically to the voting rights address—far more

than were received in response to any other speech President Johnson delivered; in addition, during the month following the address, the White House received more than 36,000 messages responding to the president's actions on civil rights, the situation in Selma, and the voting rights bill. A clear majority of the responses (greater than ninety-four percent) are favorable, and most of the unfavorable messages express negative attitudes about the Selma demonstrations and federal legislation rather than the address itself.[1]

Public and Personal Reactions

Most of the responses to President Johnson's message communicated general praise, calling it forceful, moving, and persuasive. Many newspapers and magazines proclaimed that this was LBJ's best address, while others went so far as to call it the best one by any U.S. president on the issue of race. *Time* magazine claimed that the speech was "so startling, so moving, that few who saw or heard it will ever forget it." The *Washington Star* called the address a "masterful mixture of rhetoric and eloquence." The *Christian Science Monitor* lauded it as "a landmark," and even the *Nation* and the *Spectator* (London)—two periodicals usually reserved in their praise for LBJ—labeled it "splendid." The *New Republic,* usually critical of the president's policies, declared that the address was "a moving performance" and "the best we ever heard him give." *Newsweek* contended that Johnson's words "were the strongest ever spoken by a U.S. President on the agonizing problem of race." Similarly, the *Minneapolis Spokesman* stated, "No other President speaking to Congress and the American people has ever before so honestly, unequivocally, and courageously laid the issue so squarely and fully on the line." And the influential European newspaper *Neue Zürcher Zeitung* (Zurich) emphasized that no president had expressed the same "inner strength, compassion, and energy" as LBJ.[2]

African American newspapers and leaders generally concurred with the assessment of the mainstream media. The *Norfolk Journal and Guide* judged the speech a "classic message" characterized by "eloquent prose." The *Kansas City Call* called it a "stirring address" and proclaimed it to be "the strongest speech on human rights ever made by any president." Martin Luther King Jr. expressed a similar sentiment in a telegram to LBJ, characterizing the address as "the most moving eloquent, unequivocal, and passionate plea for human rights ever made by a president of this nation." SNCC chair John Lewis congratulated the president in a personal letter, calling the message "historic, eloquent and more than inspiring for all of us who seek to make the principles of democracy a living reality." NAACP executive secretary Roy Wilkins declared that the address was a "moment at the summit in the life of our nation." Moreover, many civil rights workers, including King and those gathered in Selma to watch the speech, were moved to tears by the president's words.[3]

Citizens who sent their personal reactions to the White House were congratulatory along similar lines. Novelist John Steinbeck praised the president's eloquence and determination, which he asserted would map "the course of the future." New York advertising executive Maxwell Dane claimed that the address represented Johnson "at his best." Texas judge Cullen Briggs regarded it as "the greatest speech since the Gettysburg address," and Saint Louis department store owner Arthur Baer claimed it "would go down in history right along side Lincoln's famous address a century ago."[4]

Still, Johnson had his detractors. Although SNCC's chair praised LBJ, its more militant executive secretary, James Forman, characterized the president's speech as "empty symbolism." Some Southerners, such as Atlanta resident F. P. Gilstrap, simply informed LBJ that they were "disappointed in [his] speech," while others called the address "idiotic" and the worst message by a U.S. president on the issue of race. For instance, Alabaman John Cranford stated baldly, "Your public statement of yesterday was the most asinine statement that I have ever heard of a person in your position making." Richmond resident C. Marion Jackson even questioned the president's sanity and urged him to "make an appointment with the nearest good psychiatrist." Even some progressive Southerners found fault: The *Atlanta Journal* praised the president's clarity and determination yet claimed that his address was "too long, too tedious, too melodramatic, too full of homilies."[5]

In addition to expressing general reactions to his rhetoric, many journalists and citizens praised President Johnson's leadership and expressed confidence that his rhetorical power and political acumen would guarantee legislative success. African American labor leader A. Philip Randolph claimed that the voting rights address represented the "highest order of moral and political statesmanship." The *New York Amsterdam News* praised Johnson for putting "the full weight of his office behind the bill." In a personal letter to the president, Supreme Court chief justice Earl Warren speculated that it must have thrilled Americans to see LBJ "pledge his faith and his action to make a reality the principle of equality before the law." Warren also decreed, "And there need be no doubt of this: you will overcome." Americans for Democratic Action (ADA) chair John Roche also expressed confidence in his personal letter lauding Johnson: "[T]he intensity of your leadership in this fight will surely turn the tide."[6]

On top of eliciting comments about the president's rhetorical achievement and political leadership, the voting rights address also educed comments about his personal convictions. Many journalists and citizens commended the speech on the grounds that it revealed the president's sincerity, sensitivity, and commitment on rights, which some—until hearing this speech—believed Johnson did not possess. The *Nation* claimed, "No one who heard the President can doubt his sincerity," while *Newsday* called LBJ's message "a personal appeal from the very heart of a President born far below the Mason-Dixon line." The *Oklahoma Journal* went so far as to maintain that the address "must have dispelled once and for all the lingering suspicion and distrust Negroes have for the Southerner." The *Sarawak Tribune* (Kuching, Malaysia) praised "the sincerity of President Johnson . . . in upholding the dignity of man and the destiny of democracy," and *Outlook* (Lagos, Nigeria) expressed confidence in the president's "sincere desire to stamp out racial bigotry." In a letter to LBJ, Mississippi journalist Philip Carter called Johnson's address "the most powerfully eloquent and convincing statement of personal and official commitment to the cause of civil rights that I have ever heard from any man in public office." And an anonymous citizen from Cambridge, Massachusetts, wrote the president, "After hearing your speech I am, for the first time, convinced that you truly do understand this racial situation . . . and that you are sincere in what you say."[7]

Similarly, many African Americans praised Johnson's speech in part because they felt it revealed a personal commitment to their cause. Though most civil rights leaders believed LBJ had personal convictions on the issue of race, many blacks—including black journalists—had been skeptical: The president's voting rights address, however, seemed to change their minds. The *Philadelphia Afro-American* called the message a "sincere and moving address." The *Norfolk Journal and Guide* reported that "President Johnson went before the nation—indeed, before the whole world—and bared . . . his heart." Jackie Robinson also praised what he took to be Johnson's expression of personal sincerity, calling the message a "historic and obviously heartfelt address." The *Pittsburgh Courier* claimed, "No one who heard the address can deny the sincerity of the man. Here is a Southerner who has broken the bonds of Southern tradition and [shown] all the world that he is great because he has a big heart." And the *Amsterdam News* reported that Johnson spoke with "devotion and . . . obvious dedication" and that the phrase "we shall overcome" "rang with gripping sincerity" from his lips.[8]

The president's critics, however, seemed divided about whether the speech was an index of his personal convictions. For example, Tennessean Gerald Wallace personally communicated (in offensive language) his belief that the president must be "a nigger and communist lover" to deliver such an address. Yet in his letter to LBJ, Kansas City resident Robert Bentley claimed the speech revealed that Johnson was acting out of political concerns "instead of being truly interested in the racial problem."[9]

Beyond praising or criticizing President Johnson's rhetorical act for what it represented, listeners also responded to and engaged his specific appeals, including his identification of voting rights with the myth of America's promise and purpose. Many journalists adopted the president's mythic frame when reporting on or editorializing about his speech. The *Cleveland Plain Dealer* reported that LBJ spoke "not only for Negroes denied the right to vote, but for the values and the purpose and the meaning of our nation." The *Christian Science Monitor* lauded him for speaking the nation's conscience, invoking God's will, and affirming "the most sacred and deeply held convictions of a nation." The *Kansas City Star* appreciated Johnson's emphasis on fundamental American principles and commitments, which it claimed "brought the present chapter in the struggle for American rights into proper perspective." Furthermore, the *Chicago Defender* commended Johnson for interweaving the destiny of the United States with "the destiny of the American Negro." Several newspapers, including the *Afro-American,* proclaimed that, by awakening the nation's conscience and recommitting the United States to its purpose, Johnson had helped ensure the passage of voting rights legislation. In perhaps the most fervent response to the president challenging the nation to live up to its purpose and promise during this time of trial, the *New York Times* asserted, "A people that has responded unflinchingly to every trial of national purpose, whether in way, economic disaster or readiness to aid the afflicted abroad, will not fail this test."[10]

Many listeners also responded positively to Johnson's depiction of the civil rights movement. His strategy of praising the activists had been risky since it identified him with the movement—toward which many Americans were ambivalent. Not surprisingly, most African Americans were especially pleased by this identification. The *Norfolk Journal and Guide* praised LBJ for having endowed the civil rights movement "with the influence and prestige of the office of the President of the United States." SCLC director C. T. Vivian claimed that Johnson's speech was "a victory like none other; it was an affirmation of the movement." However, even publications that had at times expressed some concern about the tactics of the civil rights movement supported the president's depiction. For example, the *New York Times* lauded LBJ for having "hailed the Negro as 'the real hero' in the struggle to make freedom secure and meaningful for all Americans," and the *New Republic* claimed, "It took guts to come out and say 'the real hero of the struggle is the American Negro.'" In addition, since President Johnson's positive depiction of the movement focused on its goals, it is significant that several responses to his address suggest his portrayal was cogent and forceful. For instance, the *Christian Science Monitor* stated that the president had "made the Negroes' hopes and demands both clearer and more persuasive to his white fellow Americans."[11]

In contrast, many Southerners were critical of Johnson's strong identification with the movement, especially his use of the phrase "We shall overcome." For example, a member of Congress from North Carolina expressed his shock to a reporter for the *Greensboro* (North Carolina) *Daily News* that the president had adopted "the theme song of the 'radicals.'"[12]

Other reactions suggest that some listeners also found the president's claims regarding the regional frictions created by the issue of civil rights to be persuasive. Though few attended to the president's claim that civil rights problems are not confined to the South but rather exist throughout the nation, Morris Abram, president of the American Jewish Committee, wrote to Johnson to concur with his judgment: "We agree that this is an American problem rather than a sectional one." Even the *Greensboro Daily News* expressed guarded support for Johnson for having made his "moral demand upon all the American people, North and South." Regarding President Johnson's call for a New South, the *Washington Star* commended him for urging whites in the region to let go of the past for the sake of their own future, while ABC News correspondent Malvin Goode praised the president for giving assurance to those white Southerners who already want "to break away from this tradition." With regard to LBJ's claim that Southerners' concerns about states' rights were misplaced, an article in the *Parsons* (Kansas) *Sun* suggests his claim was compelling: "[H]is terms are such as to remove all legitimate fears held by many about massive federal intervention in the electoral affairs of all states. Indeed, federal intervention will be quite unnecessary if the states do their lawful duty."[13]

Finally, a significant number of listeners seem to have been persuaded by Johnson's claims that aimed to refashion their sense of time, as many journalists praised the address as being timely and appropriate for the occasion. For example, the *Amsterdam News* applauded its "historical timeliness," while UPI correspondent Helen Thomas simply reported, "The occasion demanded a supreme effort. . . . President

Johnson rose to the occasion." The *Nation* claimed that, although LBJ had previously struggled to keep from being overrun by an agitated public, by the time of the speech, "he sensed the mood" and "came to life" and exhibited "leadership worthy of the occasion." The *Kansas City Call* also addressed previous concerns about Johnson's timing: "Those who have said that President Johnson was slow in taking a stand on the Selma situation must have the feeling now that what the chief executive said Monday night was worth waiting for." In addition to claiming that "the same phrases ten days ago might have fallen flat," the *Parsons Sun* asserted that the president's perfect timing would "insure a prompt and affirmative response" from Congress and head off a filibuster or other delays.[14]

Yet some Southerners characterized the speech as hysterical and claimed Johnson was moving too quickly on civil rights sheerly for reasons of expediency. The *Montgomery Advertiser* criticized him for advocating "frenzied enactment of a new voting rights bill," while the *Richmond Times–Dispatch* argued the president aimed to reap political gain from the "near-hysteria generated by events in Selma."[15]

Conclusion

Most of the responses to Johnson's message were general and focused on the president's toughness, emotional expressiveness, persuasiveness, and leadership. However, some of them reveal that the audience took LBJ's address to communicate important messages apart from its propositional content, though it engaged his arguments, too.

What the president's listeners said provides some insights into their expectations and the extent to which they were met. Johnson's forcefulness seemed to provide the assurance they wanted that U.S. political institutions could meet this crisis and solve the problem of voter discrimination. The president's emotional expressiveness appeared to sublimate many listeners' roused feelings. His eloquence seemed to allow them to transcend the conflict in Selma and to endow the process of political change with dignity. His expression of personal conviction about racial justice seemed to many people an embodiment of moral leadership that would indeed help the nation overcome its racial problems. Johnson's suggestion that acting to guarantee equal voting rights would validate the nation's promise and purpose connected with many people's sense that the violence in Selma had a deeper meaning and provided the means for Americans to feel good again by confirming the nation's deepest commitments. Johnson's portrayal of the civil rights movement made it clearer to many hearers what the activists wanted. His effort to address the regional frictions created by civil rights issues confirmed some listeners' commitments to building a new South or to helping solve racial problems outside the South. Perhaps most importantly, his message about time provided the audience with the sense that the federal government had met the crisis before it had become a complete catastrophe that could not be put right and that the president had addressed the crisis with vigor and prudence.

Conclusion

Acclaim for President Johnson's "We Shall Overcome" speech has persisted, especially as the fortieth anniversary of its utterance approached. The grand opening festivities for Jazz at Lincoln Center's new facility in 2004 included a series of live performances titled "Let Freedom Swing: A Celebration of Human Rights and Social Justice," which consisted of new musical compositions that weave the sounds of jazz around the words of renowned crusaders for civil rights. The performances included homages to the words of Martin Luther King Jr., Nelson Mandela, and—perhaps surprisingly to some listeners—Lyndon Johnson. Actress Glenn Close recited excerpts from the president's voting rights address, accompanied by music composed by Jimmy Heath, a National Endowment for the Arts Jazz Master. The performance celebrated Johnson's eloquent expression of the essential truths of American democracy.

Yet President Johnson's address is not merely an abstract articulation of the political principles of the United States. Indeed, it is more impressive when evaluated in its rhetorical context. During an unstable political exigency that constituted a crisis of confidence, Johnson encouraged the American people to extend democracy and recommit themselves to national ideals, assembled contemporary events into a historic urgency that demanded immediate political action, and reasserted the fundamental integrity of American democracy. The president's address effectively participated in a critical moment in U.S. history by reinterpreting events to help focus public attitudes, beliefs, and actions on a particular political solution to the problem of disfranchisement. Using appeals fitted to the issue, moment, and audience, he helped break the backbone of Southern resistance to black voting rights and ensure passage of one of the nation's most important civil rights laws.

Although Congress might have passed a voting rights law even if Johnson had not spoken on March 15, 1965, his address ensured the swift passage of strong legislation. The president's identification of legislation as an act of redemption focused attention on the Congress and heightened the public's sense of what was at stake—even beyond what the Selma protests had accomplished—thus creating a political climate in which prudent deliberation should be characterized by authenticity, focus, and timeliness. In this context, both houses of Congress moved quickly: The Senate passed its voting rights bill on May 26, and the House passed its statute on July 9. Following reconciliation of the two by a conference committee, the House and the Senate passed the Voting Rights Act on August 3 and 4, respectively, and LBJ signed it into law on August 6, 1965. In his remarks at the signing ceremony, President Johnson emphasized that the nation had met the challenge articulated in his voting rights speech and that it had righted a historical wrong, enacted the country's sacred principles, confirmed its promise, and would now endeavor "to fulfill the rights that we now secure."[1]

Though the Selma demonstrations have rightly received attention as a crucial part of the struggle to guarantee equal voting rights, Johnson's rhetorical leadership, which was also vital, has been undervalued. Perhaps the chief political effect of the protests in Selma was that a chronic political problem was made acute: The fact that most African Americans in Alabama could not vote was made stark, as was the fact that public officials and local citizens used violence to maintain white supremacy in electoral politics. Making these facts plain and vivid induced feelings of uneasiness and guilt for many Americans. Yet these emotions did not lead to a unified, resounding demand for comprehensive federal voting rights legislation (although some members of Congress claimed that the demonstrations pointed to the need for it). The problem of voter discrimination in Selma was awful, but to some Americans it likely seemed isolated. The violence in Selma was appalling, but to some Americans it probably seemed in part the result of aggressive demonstrations. Further, many Americans seemed to believe that the problems of disfranchisement and violence could be solved if the president would act forcefully to protect African Americans and prosecute instances of voter discrimination. Indeed, the demand that the president "send a company of military police or a force of federal marshals to Selma" was at least equal to that for federal legislation.[2] A key political effect of Lyndon Johnson's speech was that many of his listeners accepted an interpretation of the exigency that seemed to insist on immediate passage of comprehensive federal voting rights legislation. LBJ's rhetoric reconfigured the political context already shaped by protest: It suggested that the crisis in Selma was both representative of the voting rights problem and a matter of grave national consequence; that the Selma protests were peaceful and sound; and that existing laws, however well enforced, would never guarantee equal access to the ballot box. Seizing the rhetorical opportunity made available by demonstrations, the president skillfully used persuasion to shape his listeners' perceptions of incidents and thus guided the flow of events toward his desired political end.

Achieving this end also required negotiation, compromise, coordination with interest groups, and other kinds of political maneuvering, all of which Johnson employed and at which he excelled. But it was chiefly through rhetoric that he helped guarantee swift passage of a strong legal measure. As LBJ invited listeners to view contemporary events through the lens of American mythology, he provided them with a symbolic way to right a wrong, restore order, purge their guilt, and reaffirm the nation's covenant. His interpretation of the exigency was a compelling account, spoken with conviction and told in appealing language. In grounding his appeals in American myth, he activated one of the strongest political resources a president can mobilize. Presidential scholar Erwin Hargrove claims that presidents will always invoke the strongest ideals (which myths express) in the political culture of the United States as a basis for action and that citizens and lawmakers will rise to the occasion if they believe in those ideals.[3]

Hargrove may be right, but for this process to work, presidents must choose ideals that seem—or can be made to seem—germane to the immediate issue and imbue them with a strong presence. Lyndon Johnson rallied the nation in part by arguing that the right to vote was central to America's promise and by making that promise living and meaningful in the present. His mythic appeals endowed American principles, especially that of equal voting rights, with an emotional and moral component that helped make them real for many listeners. A long-term effect of Johnson's rhetoric was that it helped change the political culture of the United States, along with the rhetoric of other political and civil rights leaders of the era, by writing African Americans and the struggle for racial justice into the story of America. In the short term, Johnson's rhetoric had the practical effect of cultivating overwhelming support for prompt enactment of the White House's voting rights bill.

LBJ's mythic rhetoric rooted in American civil religion, shaped the language of deliberation and helped establish the criteria for political judgment. Thus, the legislative wrangling in Congress became a discussion of the nation's destiny, promise, and purpose. For example, during the early stages of the House's debate over the voting rights bill, Rep. William Ryan (D-New York) identified the franchise as central to the nation's mission and claimed that "Congress must fulfill this mission by passing a bill which fully insures that every American . . . has the right to vote." As deliberations continued, so too did the repetition of language similar to the president's. For instance, Rep. Harold Donohue (D-Massachusetts) called the White House bill a step "along this nation's honored march toward further fulfillment of our traditional goals of equal opportunity and equal treatment for all Americans." Rep. Edward Roybal (D-California) argued that passing the measure would be for the United States "to make good on its promise . . . [to] fulfill the revolutionary dream of freedom and equality for all Americans." And Sen. John Cooper (R-Kentucky) claimed that it was the "moral duty of Congress to act" to ensure equal voting rights. Public opinion leaders also advocated legislative action in terms similar to the president's. For example, immediately after Johnson's speech, influential newspaper columnist Walter Lippmann urged Congress to pass the voting rights bill as an act of national redemption: "This time and in this case the issue of civil rights is clear as crystal. . . . Selma is not only an American tragedy. It is an American disgrace. . . . Unless Selma is expunged by a mighty national act of repentance and reparation, how shall Americans look themselves in the face when they get up in the morning?" Even opponents of the bill seemed to accept Johnson's interpretive frame: For instance, Rep. Charles Bennett (D-Florida) claimed that the United States' purpose is to ensure equal voting rights but argued that the present bill did not "accomplish that purpose." And so, even though they claimed it was unconstitutional, intended "to punish the South," and unnecessary, most opponents resigned themselves to the fact "that President Johnson's Reconstruction bill will be enacted," likely believing it was futile to mount a campaign against a measure that so many claimed was necessary to keep the American promise.[4]

Johnson's rhetoric may have led some legislators to change their minds, as a few members of Congress previously opposed to voting rights legislation came to support the White House's proposal. Yet, perhaps more importantly, his rhetoric helped create a political context in which it became more difficult for legislators to justify their opposition to the voting rights bill. Since the dominant meaning of the statute was bound up with fundamental American principles and the nation's purpose, its adversaries bore the burden of demonstrating that their opposition was not fundamentally un-American and would not cause unnecessary delay during a moment that demanded haste. This burden, combined with the fact that Johnson had put his personal credibility on the line and expressed his message with such conviction, helped demoralize the opponents of the legislation.

Furthermore, the president's arguments about the problem of voter discrimination, its causes, and its solution helped cultivate support and undercut his opposition. LBJ emphasized that voter discrimination in the South was racially discriminatory per se, declined to introduce the idea that some forms of voting restrictions are acceptable, and focused on the act of voter discrimination rather than the intentions of Southern lawmakers and voting registrars. In doing so, he put the supporters of discriminatory voting practices on the defensive. He emphasized that the current problem was caused by the shortcomings of the civil rights laws passed during the past decade, which suggested the nation had already made a commitment to voting rights that it had not realized and implied a kind of trajectory toward the achievement of equal voting. LBJ emphasized that his legislative solution to the problem of voter discrimination could be avoided if states would act on their own to establish fair elections, which checked claims that he aimed to punish the Southern states and wanted to exercise federal hegemony over Dixieland.

In addition to the rhetorical force generated by his arguments focused on the right to vote, Johnson's expansive claims about social justice were inspirational and more appealing than those presented by the opposition. The president's speech was optimistic and presented a vision of a better nation, true to its purpose and desirous of fulfilling its potential. In contrast, opponents of voting rights legislation seemed negative and narrow minded. LBJ looked toward the future. His opponents seemed mired in the past. And, coming after a dark episode such as "Bloody Sunday," Johnson's brightness was especially compelling: Most listeners found his idealistic expression of shared ideals and his invitation to advance the American Dream to be a stirring summons.

Still, the address had its limitations. For example, by neglecting to establish the protection of civil rights workers as a general legislative goal, Johnson virtually assured that Congress would not develop such a provision. He could also have bolstered his claims about the importance of time by emphasizing the long history of African Americans' efforts to secure the franchise. He might also have consoled civil rights workers and abated militant activists' skepticism toward him by including the death of Jimmie Lee Jackson in his account of the protests in central Alabama.

Another limitation of the speech is that, although Johnson's rhetoric is moralistic and rooted in Judeo-Christian values, he—perhaps surprisingly—condemns only the act of voter discrimination and not its underlying cause: racial prejudice. This rhetorical strategy may reflect his understanding of public sentiment at the time—that although most Americans supported civil rights, a significant number of whites still held prejudicial attitudes toward African Americans. In general, public opinion research suggests that many whites, including those outside the South, were averse to personal (especially social) interaction with blacks and in some aspects regarded them as inferior. Still, many whites, especially those outside the South, supported legislation providing for desegregation. Moreover, since equal voting rights would not lead to the outcome that many whites feared in regard to racial matters—increased personal interaction between the races—one would predict even higher levels of support for voting rights legislation, which indeed was the case, even among Southerners.[5] Therefore, Johnson and his speechwriters likely reasoned that decrying prejudicial attitudes would alienate some listeners and offer little benefit for passing voting rights legislation. The principle of equal voting rights transcended the conflict of racial attitudes, especially since LBJ made national character rather than personal ethics the grounds for moral judgment. Rather than attempting to elicit from his listeners feelings of guilt about their racial attitudes, he appealed to preexisting guilt about the violence against U.S. citizens and offered a way to purge it.

Since the subject of Johnson's speech was a racial matter, perhaps he should have decried racial prejudice. However, does the task of providing moral leadership on civil rights issues require that the president attempt to change his audience's racial attitudes? In this case, attempting to change people's hearts might have jeopardized the passage of the Voting Rights Act, which has provided real benefits to minority voters. Unlike desegregation measures, though, this law had little potential to create new attitudes of the heart regarding matters of race. Still, Johnson promoted a more just polity where even a divided citizenry can possess mutual respect rooted in the law and shared political principles.

President Johnson's form of moral leadership aimed to help build a better state, not a beloved community.

Using rhetoric to help the United States achieve fellowship among its citizens is a noble presidential goal and may be one that most Americans would support in the abstract. Nonetheless, on specific matters of moral controversy, one would imagine that few Americans want the president to moralize in ways that challenge their personal ethics. As the nation has become more pluralistic, it has become increasingly difficult to find a shared moral vocabulary on public affairs of the heart—a fact that explains, in part, LBJ's decision to emphasize citizens' commitments to their nation rather than their private moral beliefs. Yet if presidents cannot invoke a shared vocabulary on such affairs, perhaps they can take a first step toward building a more cohesive community by encouraging dialogue among citizens that might yield a shared moral language. Presidential efforts to change political policies and structures represent an important kind of leadership in the struggle to achieve racial justice, but a fully just society will be brought about only when people are motivated to live in closer fellowship. Despite Johnson's expressed desire to end hatred, promote love, and advance fellowship, his rhetoric did little to achieve those goals.

Although limited in its reach, Lyndon Johnson's "We Shall Overcome" speech remains a remarkable rhetorical achievement. The president skillfully used the available means of persuasion to influence a complex configuration of events, people, and ideas to help accomplish a greater good—the passage of milestone civil rights legislation, which led to substantial increases in African American electoral participation and helped empower racial minorities.[6] Some sections of the Voting Rights Act (those requiring federal approval of changes in state voting procedures, authorizing federal examiners and observers, and protecting language minorities) must be renewed by Congress: The most recent congressional extension of these provisions expires in 2007. As future sessions of Congress deliberate the means for guaranteeing equal voting rights, we should hope that future presidents will look to President Johnson's speech as an eloquent expression of principle and a model of rhetorical leadership. Given that the deliberations about voting rights in Congress and the courts have come to be characterized by acrimony and wrangling, public deliberation would benefit from an eloquent presidential message—one reaffirming the principle of equal voting rights and committing the nation to addressing new political challenges and opportunities.[7]

Notes

Introduction

1. Martin Luther King Jr. to Lyndon B. Johnson, Mar. 16, 1965, White House Central Files, EX SP2–3/1965/HU2–7, Box 68, Lyndon B. Johnson Library; "Top 100 American Speeches of the 20th Century," *University Communications,* Office of News and Public Affairs, University of Wisconsin–Madison, July 9, 2002, http://www.news.wisc.edu/misc/speeches/. In addition to being a significant rhetorical document, Johnson's speech was treated almost immediately as a major historical document and remains so today. In 1965 MGM Records and Spoken Arts, Inc., released an audio recording of the speech on LP record. Currently, the U.S. State Department's Office of International Programs includes the full text of the speech in the civil rights section of its "Basic Readings in U.S. Democracy," aimed at educating foreigners interested in U.S. political history. "The American Promise," *Basic Readings in U.S. Democracy, Pt. IV: On the Road from Slavery to Freedom,* Office of International Programs, U.S. Department of State, July 10, 2002, http://www.usinfo .state.gov/usa/infousa/facts/democrac/40.htm.
2. Robert Dallek, *Flawed Giant: Lyndon Johnson and His Times, 1961–1973,* 218–20; Robert A. Caro, *The Years of Lyndon Johnson: Means of Ascent,* xix–xxi.
3. Eugene E. White, *The Context of Human Discourse: A Configurational Criticism of Rhetoric,* 35.

Chapter One

1. U.S. House of Representatives, Committee on the Judiciary, *Debate on Articles of Impeachment: Hearings of the Committee on the Judiciary,* 93rd Congr., 2nd sess., July 25, 1974, 111; Alexander Hamilton, James Madison, and John Jay, *The Federalist,* ed. Benjamin Fletcher Wright (Cambridge: Harvard University Press, 1961), 384, 371.
2. Alexander Keyssar, *The Right to Vote: The Contested History of Democracy in the United States,* 24.
3. James Madison, *The Debates in the Federal Convention of 1787 Which Framed the Constitution of the United States of America,* ed. Gaillard Hunt

and James Brown Scott (New York: Oxford University Press, 1920), 352; Chilton Williamson, *American Suffrage: From Property to Democracy, 1760–1860*, 125.

4. Madison, *Debates*, 353–55.

5. Kirk Porter, *A History of Suffrage in the United States*, 40–41.

6. Eric Foner, *Reconstruction: America's Unfinished Revolution, 1863–1877*, 244–45.

7. Richard Claude, *The Supreme Court and the Electoral Process*, 30.

8. John Hope Franklin, *Reconstruction: After the Civil War*, 80.

9. Foner, *Reconstruction*, 277.

10. Ibid., 446.

11. Keyssar, *The Right to Vote*, 99; Foner, *Reconstruction*, 446.

12. *Minor v. Happersett*, 88 U.S. 162 (1875).

13. Robert M. Goldman, *Reconstruction and Black Suffrage: Losing the Vote in Reese and Cruikshank*, 124–25.

14. Keyssar, *The Right to Vote*, 108–11; Michael Perman, *Struggle for Mastery: Disfranchisement in the South, 1888–1908*, 41.

15. *Williams v. Mississippi*, 170 U.S. 213 (1898).

16. *Guinn v. United States*, 238 U.S. 347 (1915).

17. *Lane v. Wilson*, 307 U.S. 268 (1939).

18. *United States v. Classic*, 313 U.S. 299 (1941).

19. *Smith v. Allwright*, 321 U.S. 649 (1944).

20. J. A. Rogers, "Boswell Amendment Latest in a Series to Legally Disfranchise Negroes," *Pittsburgh Courier*, Nov. 23, 1946, 6.

21. For instance, in January 1944, a group of twenty-seven prominent civil rights advocates called for "legislation and . . . vigorous criminal prosecution by the Justice Department to protect and secure voting as a fundamental right of citizenship." "A Declaration of the Negro Voter," *Crisis*, Jan. 1944, 16–17.

22. Harry S. Truman, *Public Papers of the Presidents of the United States: Harry S. Truman, 1947*, 312, 9; Harry S. Truman, *Public Papers of the Presidents of the United States: Harry S. Truman, 1948*, 3.

23. Truman, *Public Papers of the Presidents of the United States: Harry S. Truman, 1948*, 125.

24. *Brown v. Board of Education*, 347 U.S. 483 (1954).

25. Robert Frederick Burk, *The Eisenhower Administration and Black Civil Rights*, 205; Dwight D. Eisenhower, *Public Papers of the Presidents of the United States: Dwight D. Eisenhower, 1957*, 134.

26. Martin Luther King Jr., "Give Us the Ballot" address at the May 17, 1957, prayer pilgrimage for freedom, Martin Luther King Jr., Papers Project, Stanford University.

27. Eisenhower, *Public Papers of the Presidents of the United States, 1957*, 545, 433.

28. Robert A. Caro, *The Years of Lyndon Johnson: Master of the Senate*, 1002.

29. U.S. Commission on Civil Rights, *Report of the United States Commission on Civil Rights*, 133–35; Margaret Price, *The Negro and the Ballot in the South*.

30. Dwight D. Eisenhower, *Public Papers of the Presidents of the United States: Dwight D. Eisenhower, 1960*, 14.

31. John F. Kennedy, *Public Papers of the Presidents of the United States: John F. Kennedy, 1961*, 22.

32. Steven F. Lawson, *Black Ballots: Voting Rights in the South, 1944–1969*, 267–71; U.S. Commission on Civil Rights, *Voting: 1961 Commission on Civil Rights Report*, 5.

33. John F. Kennedy, *Public Papers of the Presidents of the United States: John F. Kennedy, 1962*, 8.

34. "Report on the Progress of Civil Rights by the Attorney General Robert Kennedy to the President," Jan. 24, 1963, Burke Marshall Papers, Box 16, John F. Kennedy Library; John F. Kennedy, *Public Papers of the Presidents of the United States: John F. Kennedy, 1963*, 224.

35. U.S. Commission on Civil Rights, *Civil Rights '63: 1963 Report of the United States Commission on Civil Rights*, 15, 22, 30, 29.

36. "Task Force Issue Paper: Civil Rights," June 17, 1964, White House Central Files, Office Files of Bill Moyers, Box 94, Lyndon B. Johnson Library.

37. U.S. Commission on Civil Rights, *The Voting Rights Act: Unfulfilled Goals*, 1.

Chapter Two

1. Lyndon B. Johnson, *Public Papers of the Presidents of the United States: Lyndon B. Johnson, 1965*, vol. 2, 841–42.

2. Peter M. Bergman, *The Chronological History of the Negro in the United States*, 491, 547.

3. Harvard Sitkoff, *The Struggle for Black Equality, 1954–1992*, 34.

4. John Dittmer, *Local People: The Struggle for Civil Rights in Mississippi*, 200–07; Charles M. Payne, *I've Got the Light of Freedom: The Organizing Tradition and the Mississippi Freedom Struggle*, 294–98.

5. John R. Fry, "The Voter-registration Drive in Selma, Alabama," *Presbyterian Life*, Jan. 15, 1964, 12–22; Robert Weisbrot, *Freedom Bound: A History of America's Civil Rights Movement*, 128–29; Bruce Gordon, Field Report on Selma, Alabama, Nov. 9, 1963, Student Nonviolent

Coordinating Committee Papers, King Center Library and Archives, Atlanta, GA.

6. Howard Zinn, *SNCC: The New Abolitionists*, 149–66; Taylor Branch, *Pillar of Fire: America in the King Years, 1963–65*, 151–52; James Forman, *The Making of Black Revolutionaries*, 349–52.

7. Jerry DeMuth, "Total Segregation: Black Belt, Alabama," *Commonweal*, Aug. 7, 1964, 537; John Lewis and Michael D'Orso, *Walking with the Wind: A Memoir of the Movement*, 302.

8. U.S. Department of Justice, *Annual Report of the Attorney General of the United States, 1964*, 174; U.S. Department of Justice, *Annual Report of the Attorney General of the United States, 1965*, 170; Student Nonviolent Coordinating Committee, Special Report: Justice Department Activity in Dallas County, Alabama, Feb. 25, 1965, Student Nonviolent Coordinating Committee Papers, King Center Library and Archives, Atlanta, GA.

9. Amelia Boynton to Martin Luther King Jr., Oct. 8, 1964, Papers of Martin Luther King Jr., Series I, Box 21, King Center Library and Archives; David J. Garrow, *Bearing the Cross: Martin Luther King Jr. and the Southern Christian Leadership Conference*, 358–59.

10. Andrew Young, *An Easy Burden: The Civil Rights Movement and the Transformation of America*, 338; Ralph David Abernathy, *And the Walls Came Tumbling Down: An Autobiography*, 300; Adam Fairclough, *To Redeem the Soul of America: The Southern Christian Leadership Conference and Martin Luther King Jr.*, 226–27.

11. Lee White to Lyndon B. Johnson, Dec. 18, 1964, Appointment File (Diary Backup), Box 12, Lyndon B. Johnson Library; Clayborne Carson, ed., *The Autobiography of Martin Luther King Jr.*, 270–71; Lyndon B. Johnson to Martin Luther King Jr., Jan. 15, 1965, Tape WH6501.04, Program No. 2, Recordings of Telephone Conversations, Lyndon B. Johnson Library, Austin TX.

12. U.S. Commission on Civil Rights, *Report of the United States Commission on Civil Rights*, 92; U.S. Commission on Civil Rights, *Voting*, 27; U.S. House of Representatives, Committee on the Judiciary, *Voting Rights: Hearings on H.R. 6400 and Other Proposals to Enforce the 15th Amendment to the Constitution of the United States*, 89th Congr., 1st sess., Mar. 18, 1965, 5–8.

13. "The Effect of the Voting Rights Act," Introduction to Federal Voting Rights Laws, Civil Rights Division, U.S. Department of Justice, May 30, 2002, http://www.usdoj.gov/crt/voting/intro/intro_c.htm.

14. "Dr. King Due to Head Alabama Vote Drive," *New York Times*, Jan. 2, 1965, 16. Many business leaders also hoped to neutralize the protests through restraint and careful planning. An editorial writer for the *Selma Times–*

Journal suggested that such a strategy would confound King and end the campaign. "A Matter of Satisfaction," *Selma Times–Journal,* Jan. 6, 1965, 4.

15. "Group Arrives for Courthouse Registration," *Selma Times–Journal,* Jan. 18, 1965, 1, 5; Charles E. Fager, *Selma, 1965,* 31.

16. John Herbers, "67 Negroes Jailed in Alabama Drive," *New York Times,* Jan. 20, 1965, 1; John Herbers, "Woman Punches Alabama Sheriff," *New York Times,* Jan. 26, 1965, 19.

17. Howard James, "Selma Showdown Dramatizes Negro Drive," *Christian Science Monitor,* Feb. 3, 1965, 1; John Herbers, "Dr. King and 770 Others Seized in Alabama Protest," *New York Times,* Feb. 2, 1965, 1, 15; "270, Including King Arrested Here for Parade Violation," *Selma Times–Journal,* Feb. 1, 1965, 1, 5; "More Arrests Made in Rights Movement," *Selma Times– Journal,* Feb. 2, 1965, 1–2.

18. Garrow, *Bearing the Cross,* 389; "A Time for Decision," *Selma Times– Journal,* Feb. 11, 1965, 1; John Herbers, "Voting Is Crux of Civil Rights Hopes," *New York Times,* Feb. 14, 1965, E5.

19. "Negro Voting Rights," *Congressional Quarterly Weekly Report* 23(8) (1965): 269.

20. Branch, *Pillar of Fire,* 592–93; Fager, *Selma, 1965,* 73–74; John Herbers, "Negroes Beaten in Alabama Riot," *New York Times,* Feb. 19, 1965, 29; David Riley, "Who Is Jimmie Lee Jackson?" *New Republic,* Apr. 3, 1965, 8–9.

21. Lee White to Lyndon Johnson, Mar. 4, 1965, White House Central Files, LE/HU2–7, Box 66, Lyndon B. Johnson Library. At the same moment that the Justice Department finalized its voting rights bill, the department learned that its intervention in SCLC's suit against the Dallas County Board of Registrars had yielded results. On March 5 Judge Thomas issued an order telling the board to mail all rejected application forms to the applicants, identify the reason for rejection, and offer them an opportunity to appeal the rejection to Judge Thomas's clerk.

22. Garrow, *Bearing the Cross,* 394–97; Young, *An Easy Burden,* 354; Abernathy, *And the Walls Came Tumbling Down,* 327–29; Carson, ed., *The Autobiography of Martin Luther King Jr.,* 279; Fager, *Selma, 1965,* 85–90; "Negroes' March to Montgomery Planned Sunday," *Selma Times–Journal,* Mar. 4, 1965, 1; David J. Garrow, *Protest at Selma: Martin Luther King Jr. and the Voting Rights Act of 1965,* 66–73.

23. Testimony from *Hosea Williams, John Lewis et al. v. George Wallace, Governor of Alabama et al.,* NRCA-21-ANMCVCA-2181-TESTMNY, NARA Southeast Region, National Archives; Roy Reed, "Alabama Police Use Gas and Clubs to Rout Negroes," *New York Times,* Mar. 8, 1965, 20; "Civil Rights Leader Will Seek Sanction of Court for March," *Selma Times–Journal,* Mar. 8, 1965, 1–2.

24. Testimony from Hosea Williams; Lewis and D'Orso, *Walking with the Wind*, 327–30; Garrow, *Protest at Selma*, 73–76; Reed, "Alabama Police Use Gas and Clubs to Rout Negroes," 20; Warren Hinkle and David Welsh, "Five Battles of Selma," *Ramparts*, June 1965, 26–28.

25. Sasha Torres, *Black, White, and in Color: Television and Civil Rights*, 33.

26. "Incident at Selma," *New York Times*, Mar. 9, 1965, 65; "The Bridge at Selma," *Christian Science Monitor*, Mar. 12, 1965, 16; "Selma—an Assessment," *Christian Science Monitor*, Mar. 15, 1965, 14; Erwin Canham, "Selma Shock Waves," *Christian Science Monitor*, Mar. 11, 1965, 18; "Thousands across Nation Hold Sympathy Marches," *New York Times*, Mar. 10, 1965, 1; "Impact and Anger," *Newsweek*, Mar. 22, 1965, 21–22; "Selma Stirs Protests across the Nation," *New York Times*, Mar. 14, 1965, 64.

27. U.S. Information Agency, "World Press Reaction to Selma," Mar. 29, 1965; Office of Research Reports: 1964–1974, Folder R-35-65, National Archives.

28. Young, *An Easy Burden*, 360; Abernathy, *And the Walls Came Tumbling Down*, 337–40; Fager, *Selma, 1965*, 102–5; "Voting Rights Developments," *Congressional Quarterly Weekly Report* 23(11) (1965): 377; David C. Taylor, writer and prod., *Crossing the Bridge* [documentary] (New York: A&E Television Networks, 2001).

29. "Selma—an Assessment," 14; Canham, "Selma Shock Waves," 18; Nan Robertson, "Johnson Pressed for a Voting Law," *New York Times*, Mar. 9, 1965, 1; Saville R. Davis, "Negroes near Goal," *Christian Science Monitor*, Mar. 11, 1965, 1.

30. "Johnson Remarks Taken Favorably," *New York Times*, Mar. 14, 1965, 64; Lyndon B. Johnson, *Vantage Point: Perspectives of the Presidency, 1963–1969*, 162.

Chapter Three

1. George Reedy, *Lyndon Johnson: A Memoir*, 52; Jeffrey K. Tulis, *The Rhetorical Presidency*, 161; Theodore Otto Windt Jr., *Presidential Rhetoric: 1961 to the Present*, 52; David Zarefsky, "The Great Society as a Rhetorical Proposition," *Quarterly Journal of Speech* 65 (1979): 366; Doris Kearns, *Lyndon Johnson and the American Dream*, 217–18; Steven F. Lawson, "Civil Rights," 116.

2. Jack Valenti, interview by the author, Sept. 16, 2002; Brian Sweany, "Voting Rites," *Texas Monthly*, Mar. 2000, 63; G. Mennen Williams, memo to Lyndon B. Johnson, Dec. 4, 1963, Legislative Background: Voting Rights Act of 1965, Box 2, Lyndon B. Johnson Library; President's Commission on Registration and Voter Participation, *Report of the President's Commission on Registration and Voter Participation*, 40.

3. William E. Leuchtenberg, "The Genesis of the Great Society," 36–39; Task Force Issue Paper: Civil Rights, June 17, 1964, Office Files of Bill Moyers, Box 94, Lyndon B. Johnson Library.

4. Eric F. Goldman, *The Tragedy of Lyndon Johnson*, 318; Lee White to Lyndon Johnson, Nov. 18, 1964, White House Central Files, HU2/MC, Box 22, Lyndon B. Johnson Library; "Civil Rights," White House Central Files, HU2, Box 3, Lyndon B. Johnson Library; Lee White to Bill Moyers, Dec. 30, 1964, Lee White Papers, Box 3, Lyndon B. Johnson Library; Kearns, *Lyndon Johnson and the American Dream*, 217–18; Irving Bernstein, *Guns or Butter: The Presidency of Lyndon Johnson*, 223; Dallek, *Flawed Giant*, 212; Mark Stern, *Calculating Visions: Kennedy, Johnson, and Civil Rights*, 216–17.

5. Louis Martin, interview by Ed Edwin, May 2, 1985, transcript, Oral History Research Office, Columbia University Libraries.

6. Louis Martin to John Bailey, Nov. 17, 1964, Legislative Background: Voting Rights Act of 1965, Box 1, Lyndon B. Johnson Library; Matthew Reese Jr. to Lyndon Johnson, Dec. 1964, Office Files of Lee White, Box 3, Lyndon B. Johnson Library; John Andrew III, *Lyndon Johnson and the Great Society*, 34.

7. Lyndon Johnson to Nicholas Katzenbach, Dec. 14, 1964, Recordings of Telephone Conversations, WH6412.02, Lyndon B. Johnson Library; Nicholas Katzenbach to Lyndon Johnson, Dec. 28, 1964, U.S. Justice Department Administrative History, vol. 7, pt. Xa, Lyndon B. Johnson Library.

8. "Civil Rights," White House Central Files, HU2, Box 3, Lyndon B. Johnson Library; Lee White to Bill Moyers, Dec. 30, 1964, Office Files of Lee White, Box 3, Lyndon B. Johnson Library.

9. Lyndon B. Johnson, *Public Papers of the Presidents of the United States: Lyndon B. Johnson, 1965*, vol. 1, 5; Robert E. Baker, "Johnson May Ask Ban on Voter Literacy Tests," *Washington Post*, Jan. 6, 1965, A1; Draft of Constitutional Amendment, Jan. 8, 1965, Legislative Background: Voting Rights Act of 1965, Box 1; Nicholas Katzenbach to Lawrence O'Brien, Jan. 11 and Jan. 18, 1965, Reports on Pending Legislation, Box 8, Lyndon B. Johnson Library.

10. "Negro Voting Rights," *Congressional Quarterly Weekly Report* 23(8) (1965): 270–71; Charles Diggs Jr. to Lyndon Johnson, Feb. 10, 1965, Legislative Background: Voting Rights Act of 1965, Box 1, Lyndon B. Johnson Library; Lee White to Charles Diggs Jr., Feb. 12, 1965, Legislative Background: Voting Rights Act of 1965, Box 1, Lyndon B. Johnson Library; Johnson, *Public Papers of the Presidents of the United States: Lyndon B. Johnson, 1965*, vol. 1, 133; John D. Pomfret, "President Promises Dr. King

Vote Move," *New York Times,* Feb. 10, 1965, 1; John D. Morris, "President to Ask Law to End Curbs of Negro Voting," *New York Times,* Feb. 7, 1965, 1. The U.S. representatives who visited Selma did indeed meet with the attorney general to discuss voting legislation on February 24.

11. Ramsey Clark to Lawrence O'Brien, Feb. 15, 1965, Reports on Pending Legislation, Box 9, Lyndon B. Johnson Library.

12. "Lyndon Johnson and the Civil Rights Revolution: A Panel Discussion," in *Lyndon Baines Johnson and the Uses of Power,* 174.

13. Rowland Evans and Robert Novak, "From Selma to Capital Hill," *Washington Post,* Feb. 15, 1965, A15; E. W. Kenworthy, "31 in G.O.P. Urge Speed on Vote Bill for Negroes," *New York Times,* Feb. 24, 1965, 28; Joseph A. Loftus, "G.O.P. Senators Prod Johnson for Safeguard on Voting Rights," *New York Times,* Feb. 27, 1965, 11; Archibald Cox to Nicholas Katzenbach, Feb. 23, 1965, Legislative Background: Voting Rights Act of 1965, Box 1, Lyndon B. Johnson Library; Lee White to Jack Valenti, Mar. 1, 1965, White House Central Files, LE/HU 2–7, Box 66, Lyndon B. Johnson Library.

14. Draft legislation, Mar. 5, 1965, U.S. Justice Department Administrative History, vol. 7, pt. Xa, Lyndon B. Johnson Library; Lee White to Lyndon Johnson, Mar. 4, 1965, White House Central Files, LE/HU 2–7, Box 66, Lyndon B. Johnson Library; "Memo on Voting Legislation," n.d., Legislative Background: Voting Rights Act of 1965, Lyndon B. Johnson Library; Garrow, *Protest at Selma,* 70–72; Charles Mohr, "Johnson, Dr. King Confer on Rights," *New York Times,* Mar. 6, 1965, 9; Harold Reis to Lee White, Mar. 5, 1965, White House Central Files, LE/HU 2–7, Box 72, Lyndon B. Johnson Library. For instance, civil rights leaders later expressed some dissatisfaction that the bill's formula for determining when to assign registrars kept it from covering Texas, Arkansas, Florida, and Tennessee and that the bill did not provide for immediate elections after federal registrars took control.

15. Robertson, "Johnson Pressed for a Voting Law," 1, 24.

16. *United States v. Mississippi,* 380 U.S. 128 (1965); *Louisiana v. United States,* 380 U.S. 145 (1965).

17. Lyndon Johnson to Lawrence O'Brien, Mar. 10, 1965, Legislative Background: Voting Rights Act of 1965, Lyndon B. Johnson Library; Lawrence O'Brien to Lyndon Johnson, Mar. 10, 1965, White House Central Files, LE/HU 2–7, Box 66, Lyndon B. Johnson Library; Lyndon Johnson to Nicholas Katzenbach, Mar. 10, 1965, Recordings of Telephone Conversations, WH6503.04, Lyndon B. Johnson Library; Johnson, *Public Papers of the Presidents of the United States: Lyndon B. Johnson, 1965,* vol. 1, 273; "Issues to Be Resolved on Voting Legislation," Mar. 11, 1965, Legislative

Background: Voting Rights Act of 1965, Lyndon B. Johnson Library; Lyndon B. Johnson to Nicholas Katzenbach, Mar. 11, 1965, Recordings of Telephone Conversations, WH6503.06, Lyndon B. Johnson Library; Eric Sevareid script, Mar. 12, 1965, "Walter Cronkite and the News," Legislative Background: Voting Rights Act of 1965, Box 1, Lyndon B. Johnson Library.

18. Ramsey Clark to Bill Moyers, Mar. 13, 1965, Office Files of Bill Moyers, Box 6, Lyndon B. Johnson Library; Barefoot Sanders to William McCulloch, Mar. 15, 1965, U.S. Justice Department Administrative History, vol. 7, pt. Xa, Lyndon B. Johnson Library; Johnson, *Public Papers of the Presidents of the United States: Lyndon B. Johnson, 1965*, vol. 1, 274–81; Garrow, *Protest at Selma*, 99–106.

Chapter Four

1. Horace Busby to Bill Moyers and Lee White, Feb. 27, Office Files of Horace Busby, Box 3, Lyndon B. Johnson Library; Harry McPherson to Lyndon Johnson, Mar. 12, 1965, Legislative Background: Voting Rights Act of 1965, Box 2, Lyndon B. Johnson Library; Bill Moyers to Lyndon Johnson, n.d., Office Files of Bill Moyers, Box 6, Lyndon B. Johnson Library; Hubert Humphrey to Lyndon Johnson, Mar. 12, 1965, Legislative Background: Voting Rights Act of 1965, Box 2, Lyndon B. Johnson Library.

2. Robert Mann, *The Walls of Jericho: Lyndon Johnson, Hubert Humphrey, Richard Russell and the Struggle for Civil Rights*, 460; Johnson, *Vantage Point*, 164–65; Halford R. Ryan, "LBJ's Voting Rights Address: Adjusting Civil Rights to the Congress and the Congress to Civil Rights," 231.

3. Jack Valenti, notes from a meeting in the Cabinet Room, Mar. 14, 1965, Appointment File (Diary Backup), Box 15, Lyndon B. Johnson Library; E. W. Kenworthy, "Johnson to Address Congress Tonight on Voting Rights Bill," *New York Times*, Mar. 15, 1965, 1.

4. Johnson, *Vantage Point*, 164.

5. Jack Valenti to Lyndon Johnson, Mar. 16, 1965, Legislative Background: Voting Rights Act of 1965, Box 1, Lyndon B. Johnson Library.

6. Diary entry, Mar. 14, 1965, President's Daily Diary, Lyndon B. Johnson Library; Jack Valenti, *A Very Human President*, 85; Jack Valenti, interview by author, Sept. 16, 2002.

7. Horace Busby, drafts, "Message on Voting Rights," Mar. 10 and 12, 1965, Office Files of Horace Busby, Box 3, Lyndon B. Johnson Library; Horace Busby, "Message on Voting Rights," n.d., Office Files of Horace Busby, Box 3, Lyndon B. Johnson Library; Horace Busby, speech draft, "Message on Voting Rights," n.d., Office Files of Horace Busby, Box 3, Lyndon B. Johnson Library.

8. Richard N. Goodwin, *Remembering America: A Voice from the Sixties,* 325–27; Bill Moyers, letter to author, July 30, 2003; Harry McPherson, letter to author, June 18, 2003.

9. Johnson, *Vantage Point: Perspectives of the Presidency, 1963–1969,* 164; Goldman, *The Tragedy of Lyndon Johnson,* 319; diary entry, Mar. 14, 1965, President's Daily Diary, Lyndon B. Johnson Library; Richard Goodwin, interview by author, Sept. 16, 2003. Goodwin may have included a passage about Johnson's experience in Cotulla even if the president had not suggested it. Bill Moyers notes that the experience was important to Johnson and a common subject of LBJ's public and private communication: "It obviously had a strong impact upon his resolve to act when he could on behalf of the disenfranchised. He would use it in a stump speech or when he was trying to persuade a member of Congress" (quoted in Jule Leininger Pycior, *LBJ and Mexican Americans: The Paradox of Power,* 141).

10. Horace Busby, speech draft, "Message on Voting Rights," n.d., Office Files of Horace Busby, Box 3, Lyndon B. Johnson Library; Lyndon B. Johnson, "Remarks of Vice President Lyndon B. Johnson, Memorial Day, Gettysburg, Pennsylvania," May 30, 1963, sound recording, Audiovisual Archives, Lyndon B. Johnson Library; Voting Record and Excerpts from Speeches of Lyndon B. Johnson on Civil Rights, n.d., Appointment File (Diary Backup), Box 14, Lyndon B. Johnson Library; Jack Rosenthal, interview by author, Jan. 23, 2004; Jack Rosenthal to Jack Valenti, Mar. 10, 1965, Office Files of Horace Busby, Box 3, Lyndon B. Johnson Library.

11. Johnson, *Public Papers of the Presidents of the United States: Lyndon B. Johnson, 1965,* vol. 1, 274–75; draft statements, President's News Conference of Mar. 13, 1965, White House Press Office Files, Box 71, Lyndon B. Johnson Library.

12. Speech drafts, President's Remarks to Accompany Voting Message, Mar. 15, 1965, Statements of LBJ, Box 141, Lyndon B. Johnson Library; Johnson, *Vantage Point,* 164–65; Lady Bird Johnson, *A White House Diary,* 252–53.

13. Reading copy, Special Message to the Congress: The American Promise, Mar. 15, 1965, Statements of LBJ, Box 141, Lyndon B. Johnson Library. All of the quotes from the delivered version of President Johnson's address come from the author's transcription of an audio recording of the speech kept in the archives of the Johnson Library, President Johnson's Voting Rights Address, Mar. 15, 1965, WHCA 269/70, Audio Collection, Lyndon B. Johnson Library. In a line-by-line account of Johnson's ad-libbing, Ritter and Harlow observe that the changes reflected LBJ's goals and personal qualities, especially his desire to reach out to fellow white Southerners and congressional conservatives; his understanding of how jealously

members of Congress guarded their duty to initiate legislation; and
his own monumental ego. See Kurt Ritter and William Forrest Harlow,
"Lyndon B. Johnson's Voting Rights Address of March 15, 1965: Civil
Rights Rhetoric in the Jeremiad Tradition," 210.

14. Johnson, *Vantage Point*, 164; Richard L. Stout, " 'Rights' Protests Surge,"
Christian Science Monitor, Mar. 15, 1965, 1; Caro, *The Years of Lyndon
Johnson*, xviii.

15. Mann, *The Walls of Jericho*, 455; Johnson, *Vantage Point*, 162; Goldman,
The Tragedy of Lyndon Johnson, 318.

Chapter Five

1. Isocrates, *Isocrates*, 171; Thomas B. Farrell, *Norms of Rhetorical Culture*,
326.

2. Mircea Eliade, *The Myth of the Eternal Return*.

3. Robert N. Bellah, *Broken Covenant: American Civil Religion in a Time
of Trial*, 3; Roderick P. Hart, *The Political Pulpit*, 12; Russell B. Nye, *This
Almost Chosen People: Essays in the History of American Ideas*, 165; Richard
V. Pierard and Robert D. Linder, *Civil Religion and the Presidency*, 25.

4. Kenneth Burke, *A Grammar of Motives*, 77, 84.

5. Martin Luther King Jr., "Address to Rally before March," Feb. 2, 1965,
Papers of Martin Luther King Jr., Series III, Box 7, King Center Library
and Archives.

6. "Negro Voting Rights," *Congressional Quarterly Weekly Report* 23(8)
(1965): 270.

7. Nicholas Katzenbach to Lyndon Johnson, Mar. 13, 1965, President's
Appointment File (Diary Backup), Box 14, Lyndon B. Johnson Library;
Dan T. Carter, *The Politics of Rage: George Wallace, the Origins of the New
Conservatism, and the Transformation of American Politics*, 253–54.

8. In a conversation with President Kennedy's chief speechwriter in the
summer of 1963, Johnson made it clear that he believed it was important
for the president to make Southerners "feel that they're on the losing side
of an issue of conscience" in his civil rights rhetoric. Edison Dictaphone
Recording of a Telephone Conversation between Lyndon Johnson and
Theodore C. Sorensen, June 10, 1963, Lyndon B. Johnson Library.

9. Martin Luther King Jr., "Give Us the Ballot," May 17, 1957, Martin Luther
King Jr., Papers Project, Stanford University; Martin Luther King Jr.,
"Mass Meeting Address at Brown Chapel," Feb. 1, 1965, Papers of Martin
Luther King Jr., Series III, Box 7, King Center Library and Archives.

10. Hubert H. Humphrey, interview by Michael L. Gillette, June 21, 1977,
transcript, Oral History Collection, Lyndon B. Johnson Library; Jack

Valenti, interview by Joe B. Frantz, Oct. 18, 1969, transcript, Oral History Collection, Lyndon B. Johnson Library.

11. Lyndon B. Johnson, *Public Papers of the Presidents of the United States: Lyndon B. Johnson, 1963–1964,* vol. 1, 112–18, 704–07. The militaristic language of this excerpted passage (i.e., defining social problems as "enemies") also echoes President Johnson's antipoverty rhetoric, in which he declared "an unconditional war on poverty."

12. Ibid., vol. 2, 1281–88; Kennedy, *Public Papers of the Presidents of the United States,* 468–71; Merle Miller, *Lyndon: An Oral Biography,* 435; "The North Is Next," *Progressive,* July 1963, 3–4.

13. Marvin E. Olsen, "Perceived Legitimacy of Social Protest Actions," 299; Garrow, *Protest at Selma,* 289.

14. Kennedy, *Public Papers of the Presidents of the United States,* 471; Zarefsky, "The Great Society as a Rhetorical Proposition," 368; David Zarefsky, "Lyndon Johnson Redefines "Equal Opportunity": The Beginnings of Affirmative Action," *Central States Speech Journal* 31 (1980): 90; Johnson, *Public Papers of the Presidents of the United States, 1965,* vol. 2, 635–40.

15. Bayard Rustin, "From Protest to Politics: The Future of the Civil Rights Movement," *Commentary,* Feb. 1965, 25–31.

16. See, for example, Tulis, *The Rhetorical Presidency;* Samuel Kernell, *Going Public: New Strategies of Presidential Leadership.*

Chapter Six

1. Weekly summary of presidential mail for the following dates: Mar. 19, 1965; Mar. 26, 1965; Apr. 2, 1965; and Apr. 15, 1965. Mail Summaries, Box 1, Lyndon B. Johnson Library.

2. "Civil Rights," *Time,* Mar. 26, 1965; "Negro Voting," *Washington Star,* Mar. 16, 1965; Richard L. Strout, "Johnson Gives Pledge," *Christian Science Monitor,* Mar. 17, 1965; "The Nation Aroused," *Nation,* Mar. 29, 1965; Murray Kempton, "President Johnson's Challenge," *Spectator,* Mar. 19, 1965; "LBJ's Best," *New Republic,* Mar. 27, 1965; "The Starry Heavens—the Moral Law," *Newsweek,* Mar. 29, 1965; Cecil Newman, "A President's Finest Hour," *Minneapolis Spokesman,* Mar. 18, 1965; U.S. Information Agency, "World Press Reaction to Selma," Mar. 29, 1965, Office of Research Reports: 1964–1974, Folder R-35–65, National Archives.

3. "President Johnson's Message," *Norfolk Journal and Guide,* Mar. 27, 1965, 8; "We Shall Overcome," *Kansas City Call,* Mar. 19, 1965, 19; Martin Luther King Jr. to Lyndon Johnson, Mar. 16, 1965, White House Central Files, EX SP2–3/1965/HU2–7, Box 68, Lyndon B. Johnson Library; John Lewis to

Lyndon Johnson, Apr. 20, 1965, White House Central Files, SP2–3/1965, Box 67, Lyndon B. Johnson Library; Roy Wilkins to Lyndon Johnson, Mar. 16, 1965, White House Central Files, EX SP2–3/1965/HU2–7, Box 70, Lyndon B. Johnson Library.

4. John Steinbeck to Lyndon Johnson, Mar. 17, 1965, White House Central Files, EX SP2–3/1965/HU2–7, Box 68, Lyndon B. Johnson Library; Maxwell Dane to Bill Moyers, Mar. 16, 1965, White House Central Files, EX SP2–3/1965/HU2–7, Box 68, Lyndon B. Johnson Library; Cullen Briggs to Lyndon Johnson, Mar. 16, 1965, White House Central Files, EX SP2–3/1965/HU2–7, Box 68, Lyndon B. Johnson Library; Arthur Baer to Lyndon Johnson, Mar. 18, 1965; White House Central Files, EX SP2–3/1965/HU2–7, Box 68, Lyndon B. Johnson Library.

5. Lewis and D'Orso, *Walking with the Wind*, 340; F. P. Gilstrap to Lyndon Johnson, Mar. 17, 1965, White House Central Files, EX SP2–3/1965/HU2–7, Box 70, Lyndon B. Johnson Library; John Cranford to Lyndon Johnson, Mar. 16, 1965, White House Central Files, EX SP2–3/1965/HU2–7, Box 70, Lyndon B. Johnson Library; C. Marion Jackson to Lyndon Johnson, Mar. 15, 1965, White House Central Files, EX SP2–3/1965/HU2–7, Box 70, Lyndon B. Johnson Library; "That Constitution," *Atlanta Journal*, Mar. 16, 1965, 22.

6. A. Philip Randolph to Lyndon Johnson, Mar. 17, 1965, White House Central Files, EX SP2–3/1965/HU2–7, Box 68, Lyndon B. Johnson Library; "That Speech—LBJ Goes All the Way," *New York Amsterdam News*, Mar. 20, 1965, 2; Earl Warren to Lyndon Johnson, Mar. 19, 1965, White House Central Files, EX SP2–3/1965/HU2–7, Box 68, Lyndon B. Johnson Library; John Roche to Lyndon Johnson, Mar. 16, 1965, White House Central Files, EX SP2–3/1965/HU2–7, Box 68, Lyndon B. Johnson Library.

7. "The Nation Aroused," 321; "The Will of the Nation," *Newsday*, Mar. 17, 1965, 59; "Further than He Had to Go," *Oklahoma Journal*, Mar. 20, 1965, 6; U.S. Information Agency, "World Press Reaction to Selma"; Philip Carter to Lyndon Johnson, Mar. 16, 1965, White House Central Files, EX SP2–3/1965/HU2–7, Box 68, Lyndon B. Johnson Library; anonymous letter to Lyndon Johnson, Mar. 16, 1965, White House Central Files, EX SP2–3/1965/HU2–7, Box 68, Lyndon B. Johnson Library.

8. "President Johnson's Message," 8; "That Speech—LBJ Goes All the Way," 1; "What Selma Crusade Means," *Philadelphia Afro-American*, Mar. 27, 1965, 4; Jackie Robinson, "Three Cheers for LBJ," *Norfolk Journal and Guide*, Mar. 27, 1965, 8; "It Took a Hundred Years," *Pittsburgh Courier*, Apr. 3, 1965, 20; "We Are Overcoming," *New York Amsterdam News*, Mar. 20, 1965, 10.

9. Gerald Wallace to Lyndon Johnson, Mar. 16, 1965, White House Central Files, EX SP2–3/1965/HU2–7, Box 70, Lyndon B. Johnson Library; Robert

Bentley to Lyndon B. Johnson, Mar. 15, 1965, White House Central Files, EX SP2–3/1965/HU2–7, Box 70, Lyndon B. Johnson Library.

10. "What Selma Crusade Means," 4; "The President Speaks for All," *Cleveland Plain Dealer,* Mar. 16, 1965; "America's Conscience," *Christian Science Monitor,* Mar. 17, 1965, 14; "Mr. Johnson's Strong Call to Action," *Kansas City Star,* Mar. 16, 1965, 26; John H. Sengstacke, "A Letter to Our Readers," *Chicago Defender,* Mar. 17, 1965, 1; "We Shall Overcome," *New York Times,* Mar. 17, 1965, 44.

11. "LBJ's Best," 4; "President Johnson's Message," 8; "America's Conscience," 14; "We Shall Overcome," 44; Henry Hampton and Steve Fayer, *Voices of Freedom: An Oral History of the Civil Rights Movement from the 1950s through the 1980s,* 236.

12. "Voting Rights Proposal: N.C. Delegation Unenthusiastic," *Greensboro Daily News,* Mar. 17, 1965, A1.

13. Morris Abram to Lyndon Johnson, Mar. 16, 1965, White House Central Files, EX SP2–3/1965/HU2–7, Box 68, Lyndon B. Johnson Library; "Negro Voting," A10; Malvin Goode to Lyndon B. Johnson, Mar. 17, 1965, White House Central Files, EX SP2–3/1965/HU2–7, Box 68, Lyndon B. Johnson Library; "Making of a Leader," *Parsons Sun,* Mar. 16, 1965, 6.

14. "The Nation Aroused," 321; "We Shall Overcome," 19; "That Speech—LBJ Goes All the Way," 2; "Making of a Leader," 6; Helen Thomas, "LBJ's Speech Grasps Heartbreaks and Hopes," *Kansas City Call,* Mar. 19, 1965, 1.

15. "The True Loss," *Montgomery Advertiser,* Mar. 17, 1965, 4; "For a Sound Voting Law," *Richmond Times–Dispatch,* Mar. 17, 1965, 16.

Conclusion

1. Johnson, *Public Papers of the Presidents of the United States: Lyndon B. Johnson, 1965,* vol. 2, 811–15.

2. "The Power to Protect," *New Republic,* Mar. 20, 1965, 5.

3. Erwin C. Hargrove, *The President as Leader,* 21.

4. U.S. Congress, Senate, 89th Cong., 1st sess., *Cong. Rec.,* 111, pt. 4, 5105; pt. 14, 19200; pt. 12, 16280; pt. 4, 5223; Walter Lippmann, "Alabama Tragedy," *Greensboro Daily News,* Mar. 18, 1965, A8; U.S. Congress, Senate, 89th Cong., 1st sess., *Cong. Rec.,* 111, pt. 12, 16267; pt. 4, 5163; pt. 11, 11076; pt. 11, 11025; "The True Loss," *Montgomery Advertiser,* Mar. 17, 1965, 4.

5. William Brink and Louis Harris, *Black and White: A Study of U.S. Racial Attitudes Today,* 127, 36.

6. U.S. Commission on Civil Rights, *The Voting Rights Act*, 11.
7. Most of the contention centers on whether fair electoral participation should be measured by examining the process or the results—whether elections are nondiscriminatory or have led to roughly equal levels of political participation and representation.

Bibliography

Abernathy, Ralph David. *And the Walls Came Tumbling Down: An Autobiography.* New York: Harper Perennial, 1990.

Andrew III, John. *Lyndon Johnson and the Great Society.* Chicago: Ivan R. Dee, 1998.

Bellah, Robert N. *Broken Covenant: American Civil Religion in a Time of Trial,* 2d ed. Chicago: University of Chicago Press, 1992.

Bergman, Peter M. *The Chronological History of the Negro in the United States.* New York: Harper and Row, 1969.

Bernstein, Irving. *Guns or Butter: The Presidency of Lyndon Johnson.* New York: Oxford University Press, 1996.

Branch, Taylor. *Pillar of Fire: America in the King Years, 1963–65.* New York: Simon and Schuster, 1998.

———. *At Canaan's Edge: America in the King Years, 1965–68.* New York: Simon and Schuster, 2006.

Brink, William, and Louis Harris. *Black and White: A Study of U.S. Racial Attitudes Today.* New York: Simon and Schuster, 1967.

Burk, Robert Frederick. *The Eisenhower Administration and Black Civil Rights.* Knoxville: University of Tennessee Press, 1984.

Burke, Kenneth. *A Grammar of Motives.* Berkeley: University of California Press, 1969.

Caro, Robert A. *The Years of Lyndon Johnson: Means of Ascent.* New York: Knopf, 1990.

———. *The Years of Lyndon Johnson: Master of the Senate.* New York: Knopf, 2002.

Carson, Clayborne, ed. *The Autobiography of Martin Luther King Jr.* New York: Warner Books, 1998.

Carter, Dan T. *The Politics of Rage: George Wallace, the Origins of the New Conservatism, and the Transformation of American Politics.* Baton Rouge: Louisiana State University Press, 2000.

Claude, Richard. *The Supreme Court and the Electoral Process.* Baltimore: Johns Hopkins Press, 1970.

Dallek, Robert. *Flawed Giant: Lyndon Johnson and His Times, 1961–1973*. New York: Oxford University Press, 1998.

Dittmer, John. *Local People: The Struggle for Civil Rights in Mississippi*. Urbana: University of Illinois Press, 1994.

Eisenhower, Dwight D. *Public Papers of the Presidents of the United States: Dwight D. Eisenhower, 1957*. Washington, D.C.: GPO, 1958.

———. *Public Papers of the Presidents of the United States: Dwight D. Eisenhower, 1960*. Washington, D.C.: GPO, 1961.

Eliade, Mircea. *The Myth of the Eternal Return*. Translated by Willard R. Trask. Princeton: Princeton University Press, 1971.

Fager, Charles E. *Selma, 1965*. Boston: Beacon, 1985.

Fairclough, Adam. *To Redeem the Soul of America: The Southern Christian Leadership Conference and Martin Luther King Jr*. Athens: University of Georgia Press, 1987.

Farrell, Thomas B. *Norms of Rhetorical Culture*. New Haven: Yale University Press, 1993.

Foner, Eric. *Reconstruction: America's Unfinished Revolution, 1863–1877*. New York: Harper and Row, 1988.

Forman, James. *The Making of Black Revolutionaries*. Seattle: University of Washington Press, 1997.

Franklin, John Hope. *Reconstruction: After the Civil War*. Chicago: University of Chicago Press, 1961.

Garrow, David J. *Protest at Selma: Martin Luther King Jr. and the Voting Rights Act of 1965*. New Haven: Yale University Press, 1978.

———. *Bearing the Cross: Martin Luther King Jr. and the Southern Christian Leadership Conference*. New York: William Morrow, 1986.

Goldman, Eric F. *The Tragedy of Lyndon Johnson*. New York: Alfred A. Knopf, 1969.

Goldman, Robert M. *Reconstruction and Black Suffrage: Losing the Vote in Reese and Cruikshank*. Lawrence: University Press of Kansas, 2001.

Goodwin, Richard N. *Remembering America: A Voice from the Sixties*. Boston: Little, Brown, 1988.

Hampton, Henry, and Steve Fayer. *Voices of Freedom: An Oral History of the Civil Rights Movement from the 1950s through the 1980s*. New York: Bantam, 1990.

Hargrove, Erwin C. *The President as Leader*. Lawrence: University Press of Kansas, 1998.

Hart, Roderick P. *The Political Pulpit*. West Lafayette, IN: Purdue University Press, 1977.

Isocrates. *Isocrates,* vol. 2. Translated by George Norlin. *Loeb Classical Library*. Cambridge: Harvard University Press, 1929.

Johnson, Lady Bird. *A White House Diary*. New York: Holt, Rinehart, Winston, 1970.

Johnson, Lyndon B. *Public Papers of the Presidents of the United States: Lyndon B. Johnson, 1963–1964*, vols. 1–2. Washington, D.C.: GPO, 1965.

———. *Public Papers of the Presidents of the United States: Lyndon B. Johnson, 1965*. Vols. 1–2. Washington, D.C.: GPO, 1966.

———. *Vantage Point: Perspectives of the Presidency, 1963–1969*. New York: Holt, Rinehart, Winston, 1971.

Kearns, Doris. *Lyndon Johnson and the American Dream*. New York: Harper and Row, 1976.

Kennedy, John F. *Public Papers of the Presidents of the United States: John F. Kennedy, 1961*. Washington, D.C.: GPO, 1962.

———. *Public Papers of the Presidents of the United States: John F. Kennedy, 1962*. Washington, D.C.: GPO, 1963.

———. *Public Papers of the Presidents of the United States: John F. Kennedy, 1963*. Washington, D.C.: GPO, 1964.

Kernell, Samuel. *Going Public: New Strategies of Presidential Leadership*, 3d ed. Washington, DC: CQ Press, 1997.

Keyssar, Alexander. *The Right to Vote: The Contested History of Democracy in the United States*. New York: Basic Books, 2000.

Kotz, Nick. *Judgment Days: Lyndon Baines Johnson, Martin Luther King Jr., and the Laws That Changed America*. Boston: Houghton Mifflin, 2005.

Lawson, Steven F. *Black Ballots: Voting Rights in the South, 1944–1969*. New York: Columbia University Press, 1976.

———. "Civil Rights." In *Exploring the Johnson Years*, edited by Robert A. Divine. Austin: University of Texas Press, 1981, 93–126.

Leuchtenberg, William E. "The Genesis of the Great Society." *Reporter* (April 21, 1966): 36–39.

Lewis, John, and Michael D'Orso. *Walking with the Wind: A Memoir of the Movement*. New York: Simon and Schuster, 1998.

"Lyndon Johnson and the Civil Rights Revolution: A Panel Discussion." In *Lyndon Baines Johnson and the Uses of Power*, edited by Bernard J. Firestone and Robert C. Vogt. Westport, CT: Greenwood, 1988, 173–87.

Mann, Robert. *The Walls of Jericho: Lyndon Johnson, Hubert Humphrey, Richard Russell, and the Struggle for Civil Rights*. New York: Harcourt Brace, 1996.

Miller, Merle. *Lyndon: An Oral Biography*. New York: Putnam, 1980.

Nye, Russell B. *This Almost Chosen People: Essays in the History of American Ideas*. East Lansing: Michigan State University Press, 1966.

Olsen, Marvin E. "Perceived Legitimacy of Social Protest Actions." *Social Problems* 15 (1967): 297–310.

Payne, Charles M. *I've Got the Light of Freedom: The Organizing Tradition and the Mississippi Freedom Struggle*. Berkeley: University of California Press, 1995.

Perman, Michael. *Struggle for Mastery: Disfranchisement in the South, 1888–1908.* Chapel Hill: University of North Carolina Press, 2001.

Pierard, Richard V., and Robert D. Linder. *Civil Religion and the Presidency.* Grand Rapids: Academie Books, 1988.

Porter, Kirk. *A History of Suffrage in the United States.* Chicago: University of Chicago Press, 1918.

President's Commission on Registration and Voter Participation. *Report of the President's Commission on Registration and Voter Participation.* Washington, D.C.: GPO, 1963.

Price, Margaret. *The Negro and the Ballot in the South.* Atlanta: Southern Regional Council, 1959.

Pycior, Jule Leininger. *LBJ and Mexican Americans: The Paradox of Power.* Austin: University of Texas Press, 1997.

Reedy, George. *Lyndon Johnson: A Memoir.* New York: Andrews and McMeel, 1982.

Ritter, Kurt, and William Forrest Harlow. "Lyndon B. Johnson's Voting Rights Address of March 15, 1965: Civil Rights Rhetoric in the Jeremiad Tradition." In *Great Speeches for Criticism and Analysis,* edited by Lloyd E. Rohler. Greenwood, IN: Alistair Press, 2001, 198–219.

Ryan, Halford R. "LBJ's Voting Rights Address: Adjusting Civil Rights to the Congress and the Congress to Civil Rights." In *Contemporary American Public Discourse,* edited by Halford R. Ryan. Prospect Heights, IL: Waveland, 1992, 228–37.

Sitkoff, Harvard. *The Struggle for Black Equality, 1954–1992,* rev. ed. New York: Hill and Wang, 1993.

Stern, Mark. *Calculating Visions: Kennedy, Johnson, and Civil Rights.* New Brunswick, NJ: Rutgers University Press, 1992.

Sweany, Brian. "Voting Rites." *Texas Monthly* (March 2000): 62–67.

Torres, Sasha. *Black, White, and in Color: Television and Civil Rights.* Princeton: Princeton University Press, 2003.

Truman, Harry S. *Public Papers of the Presidents of the United States: Harry S. Truman, 1947.* Washington, D.C.: GPO, 1948.

———. *Public Papers of the Presidents of the United States: Harry S. Truman, 1948.* Washington, D.C.: GPO, 1949.

Tulis, Jeffrey K. *The Rhetorical Presidency.* Princeton: Princeton University Press, 1987.

U.S. Commission on Civil Rights. *Report of the United States Commission on Civil Rights.* Washington, D.C.: GPO, 1959.

———. *Voting: 1961 Commission on Civil Rights Report.* Washington, D.C.: GPO, 1961.

———. *Civil Rights '63: 1963 Report of the United States Commission on Civil Rights.* Washington, D.C.: GPO, 1963.

————. *The Voting Rights Act: Unfulfilled Goals.* Washington, D.C.: GPO, 1981.

U.S. Department of Justice. *Annual Report of the Attorney General of the United States, 1964.* Washington, D.C.: GPO, 1964.

————. *Annual Report of the Attorney General of the United States, 1965.* Washington, D.C.: GPO, 1965.

Valenti, Jack. *A Very Human President.* New York: Norton, 1975.

Weisbrot, Robert. *Freedom Bound: A History of America's Civil Rights Movement.* New York: Plume, 1991.

White, Eugene E. *The Context of Human Discourse: A Configurational Criticism of Rhetoric.* Columbia: University of South Carolina Press, 1992.

Williamson, Chilton. *American Suffrage: From Property to Democracy, 1760–1860.* Princeton: Princeton University Press, 1960.

Windt, Theodore Otto, Jr. *Presidential Rhetoric: 1961 to the Present,* 4th ed. Dubuque: Kendall/Hunt, 1987.

Young, Andrew. *An Easy Burden: The Civil Rights Movement and the Transformation of America.* New York: HarperCollins, 1996.

Zarefsky, David. "The Great Society as a Rhetorical Proposition." *Quarterly Journal of Speech* 65 (1979): 364–78.

————. "Lyndon Johnson Redefines 'Equal Opportunity': The Beginnings of Affirmative Action." *Central States Speech Journal* 31 (1980): 85–94.

Zinn, Howard. *SNCC: The New Abolitionists.* Boston: Beacon, 1964.

Index

ISBN-13: 978-1-58544-574-5
ISBN-10: 1-58544-574-6

52995